# The Busy Woman's Guide to Writing and Finishing a Novel

## Stop Procrastinating and Get It Done

ISBN-13:
978-1519153388

ISBN-10:
1519153384

# Table of Contents

# Why I Wrote this Book

As much as I love writing, it can be very difficult to find the time to do it. I consider raising my kids to be my main job. My youngest recently turned 1, which means he still needs a lot of my time and attention. I don't begrudge him my time, but I also want to do things for myself. My girls are homeschooled. And although we're very relaxed homeschoolers, I want to spend a lot of quality time with them.

Between kids' activities, including Girl Scouts, art class, gymnastics, choir, and park play dates, household chores, food preparation and cooking, my life is busy.

On top of that, I also work from home. I earn money by writing articles. These content articles are fun to write, but they require a lot of my time and creativity.

Yet in spite of my busy life, I published a non-fiction book about unassisted childbirth called "The Unassisted Baby", and a fiction book under my maiden name. And if I can do it, then you can do it, too! I hope this book helps you find the time to write your novel.

# Chapter 1:

# So You Wanna Write a Book, Do You?

Now that you've figured out that you want to write a book, you just joined a big group of like-minded individuals. There are about as many people who want to write a book as there are people who want to get back in shape. The good news is that you picked up the right tool to help you write the novel, although it probably won't help you lose those extra pounds.

First things first: before you get started, we have to explore a few basics. To get you to write that novel and keep writing until you're done, we need to help you uncover your motivation behind writing the book in the first place. Next, we need to help you figure out which tools you need to write a novel. After that, it's time to talk about how you can find the time you need to write.

Finally, we'll talk about all the things you'd rather be doing than writing and how to avoid giving in to the temptation. In fact, that's what this book is all about. I will help you discover enough time to write your novel, whether you have 5 kids, 2 jobs, a 3-acre garden, or all of the above.

# 1.1. Why Do You Want to Write a Book?

Everybody has a different motivation for writing their book. While some of us want to become famous, most of us have far less ambitious goals. Some people really enjoy writing and don't care whether they ever earn any money with it. Although technically speaking, even those people are hoping for somewhat of a reward, whether it's a good review, praise for writing a book, or officially becoming an author.

Of course if you don't enjoy writing, maybe you shouldn't consider writing a book. After all, writing is a lot of hard work. It takes a long time to write a book even if you don't count all of the hours you spend staring at the screen instead of actually writing. In order to keep going for the long-term, you need a really good reason to write a book.

Fortunately, the same is true for other big achievements in life. If you want to quit smoking, lose weight, or learn a new language, you'll need to draw on your inner strength to keep going when it gets tough. And let's face it, writing can be difficult. Even after you've gotten past the first few pages of your novel, it can be hard to keep going. Even Janet Evanovich, who is a bestselling author, has said: "I could write a book a month if it wasn't for the middle. I hate the middle!"[1]

---

[1] Evanovich & Yalov "How I Write – Secrets of a Bestselling Author" (2006)

So what's your motivation to write a book? Do you want to be a published author? Do you want to share the story in your head with the world? Do you love writing and seeing your name in print? Do you want to earn a living as a writer? Do you want to share your experiences with the world through your writing?

Everybody has a reason for what they do. Now it's time to find your reason to write a book. Once you find that compelling reason that will keep you going when the going gets tough, you have something to hold on to when you want to quit. If you want a visual reminder, you should write down your most important reason and hang it up above your writing area. This way you can see why you do what you do whenever you're sitting at your desk. If you can find a picture to go with it, that might be even better.

What if you can't think of any good reasons to write a book? Then you're not trying hard enough. After all, being an author comes with a lot of privileges. Here are a few examples:

- You can get payback by doing mean things to fictional characters in your book that may resemble someone who annoyed you in real life.
- You can claim that you're working when you're reading a book and call it research.
- You can claim that you're working when you're surfing the Internet and call it research.
- Wearing pants or any clothes at all is purely optional because you're a writer.

- You can live someone else's life for a change.
- Your eccentricities are now expected and no longer weird.

It's okay if you don't uncover your primary reason to write a novel today or even tomorrow. After all, it takes time to get to know your most inner motivations.

## 1.2. Uncover Your True Motivation

What motivates you to get up in the morning? What makes you happy at the end of a long workday? Chances are the answer is neither the latest TV shows nor chocolate or alcohol. While they all may sound good in the moment, none of them leads to lasting happiness or a sense of fulfillment. Plus, they usually don't provide enough good material for an inspiring eulogy or tombstone inscription.

While I don't want to be morbid, the first step to spend your time in a meaningful way is to realize that your time on Earth is limited. As Stephen Covey recommends, you should "begin with the end in mind".

True motivation is a tricky thing to uncover. But if you give it some thought, you can probably come up with one or more answers. Many people are motivated by being around people they love and doing things they enjoy. If you enjoy writing, you probably already know that.

If you can write for hours and totally get lost in the world you're creating, you're already a writer. This is true even if you haven't published a single word or only written short stories for your kids to enjoy. Unfortunately, there is a big gap between wanting to write and actually writing.

Are you ready to get started?

# Chapter 2:

# Before You Start Writing

If you already have an idea for a story, you should jot down a few notes before you forget what you were going to write. After that, it's a good idea to set yourself up for writing success by finding a place to write, choosing the right novel writing program, and clearing your calendar.

## 2.1. Find a Place to Write

Most writers have a designated area to write. Traditionally, that means having a desk set up somewhere in your home where the rest of your family will leave you alone. A lot of writers set up an office, but you certainly don't need an entire room in order to be able to write your story. Setting up a desk in the corner of your living room is just as effective. And if you don't have the space in your home, you can even put your desk inside of one of your closets (unless you suffer from claustrophobia).

Your writing space should be organized in a way that makes you feel productive. Generally, a cluttered desk overwhelms even creative individuals. Of course, if having piles of research next to your keyboard and your coffee mug motivates you to dig through it and write more, then that's the way to go for you.

Most writers will need a computer to write. However, you may still prefer to write with pen and paper. There is absolutely nothing wrong with that. The one advantage computers have is that it's much quicker to type than to write with pen and paper, and it's also a lot easier to change, delete, and rearrange the text you've written. That being said, if all you end up doing is staring at a blank screen when you work on the computer, writing by hand is still preferable. On that note, you could also write using a typewriter if you can still find one.

If you use a computer, laptop, Chromebook, tablet, or cell phone to write your novel, you'll need to find a good novel-writing program to use. That's your next step.

## 2.2. Use a Novel Writing Program

Having a computer is not enough. You also need a novel writing program to go with it. The good news is that you have lots of options. Technically, you don't need anything special to write a novel. All you need is word processing software that allows you to type. That being said, there are a few additional tools novel writers can benefit from. When you're looking at novel writing programs, you should make sure yours has the following features:

- The ability to record notes and information about your characters
- Word count (per novel, per chapter, and per scene)
- The option to outline your novel
- The functionality to reorder your scenes and chapters
- A way to track your progress (on a daily, weekly, and overall basis)

When it comes to novel writing programs, less may be more. If the program is too complicated to use, you will probably go back to using a pen and paper or your regular word processor. On the other hand, if the program is too simple, you'll end up using more than one type of program or putting sticky notes all over your desk.

## *Organizing Your Novel Details*

Organizing novel details is really important for novel writers. You have to find a way to keep track of the characters you created. After all, it's embarrassing if you misspell your character's name or change their eye color throughout the book because you can't remember what you originally chose. The more characters you have, the more important it is to save those details about each of them.

You also need to pay attention to other details you talk about in your book. Do you mention specific locations or dates? It's important to keep track of them so you can use them again later without getting them wrong.

## *Record Your Ideas Promptly*

As a writer, you can have a good idea while you're grocery shopping, putting your child to bed, or driving to work. The challenge is to find a way to record these ideas as soon as possible. If you're using a web-based novel writing program, you might even be able to record your notes while you're standing in line at the cash register.

Otherwise, you may decide to keep sticky notes or a notepad and a pen or pencil handy wherever you go. Once you get home to your writing area, you should make sure those notes get put away safely. There is nothing worse than not being able to find what you wrote in order to use it in your story.

Some authors actually like using a paper notebook alongside their computer. But if you're not into trying to read your own handwriting when it has to go fast, you're better off finding a novel writing program that incorporates a notebook. One example of such a program is Novelize (www.getnovelize.com).

## *Choose Your Medium*

Finally, you need to decide which device you're going to be working on. Will you always work on your desktop? Are you going to try to work a little bit from your work computer during lunch or on your tablet during your commute? If there's a chance you'll switch computers, it's important to select a novel writing program that's easily portable.

If you're using software, you need to download it on every computer you're planning on using. Additionally, you'll have to be extremely careful not to overwrite what you've written when you copy and paste files around. That's every writer's worst nightmare.

If you tend to switch computers, you should probably choose a web-based writing program like Novelize. On the other hand, if you have an unreliable Internet connection, it's much better to stick to a software-based program.

The good news is that no matter which program you choose, you can always change your mind if it doesn't work out for you. Plus, most writing software offers a free trial for you to test the waters.

## 2.3. Clear Your Calendar

Obviously, you're not going to do anything but write for the next 12 months. After all, you still want to have a life, talk to your family, and even spend an evening out, don't you? But the truth is that writing a novel is going to take up a lot of your valuable time. It will probably take away from your free time and family time.

If you have to work to pay rent (and who doesn't?), you'll still need to schedule time for that. Most bosses don't appreciate it if you stop coming to work because you're working on your novel. However, maybe you should say no to overtime for the foreseeable future. There are actually lots of good reasons to avoid working overtime even if you're not writing a novel:

- It takes away from family and free time.
- It leaves you feeling overworked and depleted.
- You're not actually more productive even if you spend 10 instead of 8 hours at the office.
- You might end up in a higher tax bracket. This means some of the extra money you're earning is going to Uncle Sam's pocket instead of yours.
- It makes your boss think you don't have a life.
- Working overtime makes your workdays seem endless.

There's nothing wrong with working overtime on occasion. After all, many companies have real busy seasons. An accountant probably works overtime every day from February until the middle of April. However, the rest of the year, accountants are usually a lot more relaxed and a lot less busy. In the end, it's all about balance.

Clearing your calendar doesn't mean that you should skip family birthday parties for the next few months, either. It also doesn't mean you can't go on a date, get a haircut, or visit the dentist. What I mean by clearing your calendar is that you shouldn't embark on another huge project that takes up a lot of your time.

For example, if you want to write and publish your novel within the next 6 months, you shouldn't plan on also renovating your home during that time. Chances are you can only do one or the other. Of course, this is not necessarily true if you don't need to work for a living.

# Chapter 3:

# What You Need to Know about Novel Writing

The great thing about writing a novel is that it doesn't require a degree or years of experience to do it. Granted, it takes some skill and ability to actually write a good novel, but you don't have to rely on someone else to teach you the basics.

While you may take that for granted, that's not true in most other professions. Can you imagine having a surgeon who is just kind of winging it? Not a very pleasant idea. Of course, even going through medical school, residency, and additional required learning doesn't make every surgeon a great surgeon. But that's a subject for another book (I probably won't be writing).

When it comes to novel writing, what do you need to know in order to write a novel yourself? Technically, you don't have to know much of anything. It's good if you have a good story to tell and find a good way to tell it. However, "good" is usually subjective since everybody has their own opinion about whether a book is good or not.

But if there is one thing most writers have in common, it's the fact that they love reading books. Ideally, you should write a novel in a genre that you're familiar with. If you hate reading romance novels, you might not be very good at writing that type of book. Of course, there are always exceptions to every rule, so maybe you'll create a whole new type of romance novel as a result.

Everything else you need to know about writing is some basic information that is covered next.

# 3.1. How Many Words Should Your Book Have?

Most aspiring writers wonder how many words their novel should have before they even get started. And there's nothing wrong with that. In fact, it's probably a good idea to set an overall word count goal. Once you know how long you want your novel to be, you can calculate how many words you should write each week.

## What's the Average Word Count of a Novel?

This is not an easy question to answer. The average Word count greatly depends on the type of book you're writing. Here are a few examples:

- Short stories: 1,000 – 8,000 words
- Middle grade: 20,000 to 30,000 words
- Young adult: between 40,000 and 80,000 words
- Romance novels: 40,000 – 100,000 words
- Horror: 80,000 – 100,000 words

- Historical fiction: 100,000 – 120,000 words
- Science Fiction and Fantasy: 90,000 - 125,000

These numbers are broad generalizations. It's actually not uncommon for Fantasy novels to run upwards of 200,000 words. That being said, you don't need to write that much if your story doesn't support this length.

As you'll quickly realize, every type of fiction book has a common word count range. Some genres have more flexible ranges than others. Generally, romance novels tend to be shorter than novels of historical fiction, but that doesn't mean your romance has to be short. On average, fiction books have about 64,000 words, but averages don't always matter when it comes to books or people.

You've probably read quite a few books yourself that were extremely short and some that were very long. The number of words doesn't usually give an indication of how good the book is. For example, "White Fang" by Jack London is a rather small book but extremely well written with only 72,071 words. On the other hand, "Gone with the Wind" by Margaret Mitchell has 418,053, but it keeps its readers on their toes until the very end.

## *Set a Goal and Use It to Get Going*

While you don't necessarily need to decide how many words your book is going to have, having a goal will get you going. Using a word count goal can help you calculate how many words you need to write each week in order to get your book written within the next 3, 6, or 24 months.

Another reason for having a general idea of how many words your novel should have is to flush out your story. If everything important has already happened to your main character in the first 15,000 words, you either need to come up with more ideas, get more detailed with your writing, or call it a short story.

Here is an example of what I mean by detailed writing:

"He ate breakfast because he was hungry." – That's the short version.

"He didn't even notice how long it had been since his last meal until his stomach started to growl. After carefully evaluating the contents of his empty refrigerator, he decided to prepare some scrambled eggs with a side of bacon." – This could be the longer version.

It's not necessary to elaborate on every little detail like that. After a while, your readers will get bored reading about meal preparation times. However, if it's important to your story, you should use more words to talk about it.

Including a lot of details in your writing is especially important when you're describing conflicts in your story. For example, is your hero or heroine battling internal emotions or having it out with a family member? You should spend some time talking about their feelings, anxieties, and anticipations.

Readers also like to learn more about your main characters as long as you keep things interesting. For example, you can add little anecdotes to the story about something your character did in High School. Adding extra information can make your book fun to read because it helps readers understand the type of person your main character is.

## *Focus on Developing Your Story*

As I've already explained above, you should focus on developing your story. What's going to happen next? At which point will it become impossible for your readers to stop reading because they really need to know what happens next? Obviously, the sooner you engage their interest, the better.

If you reached 90,000 words with your novel but still aren't done with your story, by all means continue. However, you can also consider breaking up your book into a series of some sort if it gets too big. Additionally, if you're going to be looking for a publisher versus self-publishing your book, then it may be necessary for you to stick to a smaller word count range at least for your first novel.

Now it's time to set your writing goals in your novel writing program. If your writing program doesn't allow you to set word count goals, you can still visualize them by putting a sticky note on your computer or bathroom mirror.

## 3.2. How Many Words Does Your Favorite Book Have?

Now that you know about the differences in overall word count between the different genres, you may wonder how many words your favorite books have. It makes sense to look at the word count of popular books because it gives you a good idea of how big your book will be when it has 50,000 words or 100,000 words. Here is a list of well-known books listed in ascending order of their respective word counts[2]:

22,416 – The Mouse and the Motorcycle – Beverly Cleary

30,644 – Charlie and the Chocolate Factory – Roald Dahl

35,968 – Old Yeller – Fred Gipson

36,363 – Lion The Witch and the Wardrobe – C.S. Lewis

46,118 – Fahrenheit 451 – Ray Bradbury

47,094 – The Great Gatsby – F. Scott Fitzgerald

47,180 – The Red Badge of Courage – Stephen Crane

59,635 – Black Beauty – Anna Sewell

59,900 – Lord of the Flies – William Golding

61,922 – All Quiet on the Western Front – Erich Remarque

63,604 – The Scarlet Letter – Nathaniel Hawthorne

63,766 – Brave New World – Aldous Huxley

64,768 – The Martian Chronicles – Ray Bradbury

---

[2] This list was retrieved from http://commonplacebook.com/culture/literature/books/word-count-for-famous-novels/.

66,556 – The Color Purple – Alice Walker
66,950 – Treasure Island – Robert Louis Stevenson
67,707 – The Sun Also Rises – Ernest Hemingway
69,066 – The Adventures of Tom Sawyer – Mark Twain
72,071 – White Fang – Jack London
73,404 – The Catcher in the Rye – J.D. Salinger
77,325 – Philosopher's Stone – JK Rowling
80,398 – The Secret Garden – Frances Hodgson Burnett
82,370 – The English Patient – Michael Ondaatje
82,762 – Anne Frank: The Diary of a Young Girl – Anne Frank
84,799 – Chamber of Secrets – JK Rowling
87,978 – Persuasion – Jane Austen
88,942 – Nineteen Eighty-Four – George Orwell
91,419 – Joy Luck Club – Amy Tan
95,022 – The Hobbit – J. R. R. Tolkien
97,364 – Anne of Green Gables – Lucy Maud Montgomery
100,609 – Ender's Game – Orson Scott Card
106,821 – Prisoner of Azkaban – JK Rowling
107,349 – Gullivers Travels – Jonathan Swift
107,945 – Wuthering Heights – Emily Bronte
109,571 – The Adventures of Huckleberry Finn – Mark Twain
112,815 – The Golden Compass – Philip Pullman
114,634 – Walden – Henry David Thoreau
119,394 – Sense and Sensibility – Jane Austen
123,378 – Atonement – Ian McEwan
127,776 – Life on the Mississippi – Mark Twain
128,886 – The Yearling – Marjorie Kinnan Rawlings
134,462 – The Return of the King – J. R. R. Tolkien
134,710 – Schindler's List – Thomas Keneally

135,420 – A Tale of Two Cities – Charles Dickens
138,138 – 20000 Leagues Under the Sea – Jules Verne
143,436 – The Two Towers – J. R. R. Tolkien
145,469 – Last of the Mohicans – James Fenimore Cooper
155,887 – Emma – Jane Austen
155,960 – Oliver Twist – Charles Dickens
156,154 – Watership Down – Richard Adams
166,622 – Uncle Tom's Cabin – Harriet Beecher Stowe
169,441 – Half Blood Prince – JK Rowling
169,481 – The Grapes of Wrath – John Steinback
174,269 – Catch-22 – Joseph Heller
177,227 – The Fellowship of the Ring – J. R. R. Tolkien
183,349 – Great Expectations – Charles Dickens
183,833 – Little Women (Books 1&2) – Louisa May Alcott
183,858 – Jane Eyre – Charlotte Brontë
186,418 – Memoirs of a Geisha – Arthur Golden
190,858 – Goblet of Fire – JK Rowling
197,517 – Stones from the River – Hegi, Ursula
198,227 – Deathly Hallows – JK Rowling
206,052 – Moby Dick – Herman Melville
211,591 – Crime and Punishment – Fyodor Dostoyevsky
225,395 – East of Eden – John Steinbeck
257,154 – Order of the Phoenix – JK Rowling
311,596 – The Fountainhead – Ayn Rand
349,736 – Anna Karenina – Leo Tolstoy
365,712 – Lonesome Dove – McMurtry, Larry
418,053 – Gone with the Wind – Margaret Mitchell
561,996 – Atlas Shrugged – Ayn Rand
587,287 – War and Peace – Leo Tolstoy

Now if you're anything like me, browsing through this list probably made you want to read or re-read some of these books. Ideally, it also makes you want to start typing, because even the shortest one has more than 22,000 words.

## 3.3. How Many Words Should You Write in a Day or Week?

Determining your overall word count goal for your novel brings us directly to the question of how many words you should write each day or each week. The tricky part is that there is no right answer to this question. Obviously, you want to write as many words as possible, because the more you write each day, the sooner you will reach the end of your novel. That being said, your goals still need to be realistic for you.

First of all, you need to decide how many days a week you're going to be writing. If you're participating in a writing sprint like National Novel Writing Month, you may be able to commit to writing 6 days a week. However, most people will be too busy to sit down almost every day to write.

The great thing is that you can easily adjust your goals. In order to set yourself up for success, you may want to start small. Commit to working on your novel for 2 or 3 days per week unless writing is your full-time job. If you find that you can easily add another day of writing, you should do it.

But if you start out trying to write 5 days each week and find that you can only manage 3, you'll be setting yourself up for disappointment. And feeling like you're not writing often enough might lead you to stop writing altogether. That's something you'll need to avoid.

So, let's get back to your word-count goals. It's a good idea to set a word count goal, especially in the beginning. In order to come up with a good daily goal, you should start by setting a total word count goal first. For example, you may want to write a book that has about 70,000 words.

Next, it's time to pick a deadline. Yes, you want to have an end in sight. When do you want this novel done by? Of course we're just talking about the first draft, but you still want to have a deadline for it. If you want the first draft done in 6 months from now, that gives you about 26 weeks to write. This means you have to write about 2,692 words every week. If you can write for 5 days each week, you only need to type 538 words each day you're writing.

Whether you want to aim for a daily goal or a weekly goal is merely a matter of preference. For example, it might sound too intimidating to write 1,000 words every day this week. You might prefer to have a total weekly word count of 3,000 words a week and commit to working at least 3 days a week. The end result is the same, but you don't feel overwhelmed.

As you start on your novel, you will get a feel for how much you can write each day. It partly depends on how much time you have to write and if you can do so without distractions. If you find out that the goal you set is unachievable, you may have to adjust it a little.

But don't forget: it's not supposed to be easy. If it was easy, everybody would do it. Plus, on some days you'll greatly exceed your daily goal because you will be on a roll and unable to stop. During those times, you might not even notice when everyone else is evacuating the town because a hurricane is coming....

## *The Importance of Setting Goals*

Wanting to write a novel is not a goal. Wanting to lose weight isn't a goal, either. Goals need to be measurable. And they have to have a deadline. Otherwise, they're just called dreams. And while there's nothing wrong with having dreams, they don't usually become reality without a little bit of effort on your part.

Having to set a specific goal for writing your book can be very intimidating. After all, setting a goal makes you vulnerable because it sets you up for failure. In fact, that's why many people are afraid to commit to setting goals. They're afraid they won't be able to reach them.

I recommend looking at it from the other side of the coin. Of course there's the possibility that you won't reach your goal. But if you don't set a goal in the first place, the likelihood of turning your dream into reality is much closer to zero than you think.

Now let's assume that you've set a goal to write your novel. But by the time the deadline rolls around, you have only managed to write half of your overall word count goal. Technically, you're entitled to feel ashamed and sorry for yourself because you didn't make it. But you can also take this as an opportunity to try again and succeed next time.

Besides, you did finish half or at least a part of your novel. That's something to be proud of. And now that you know what it's like to write regularly, you can figure out what worked best for you and tweak the things that didn't.

Ask yourself what kept you from writing during this time, and when you were most productive. Now is also a good time to figure out what helps you continue your story. Do you suffer from blank screen syndrome, or does the challenge lie in finding the time to write (we'll get to the latter problem shortly)?

When you're through feeling sorry for yourself for not meeting your goal, it's time to pick yourself up and set a new goal. And remember a goal has to be measurable with a deadline, and it needs to be in writing. Ideally, you'll share your goal with other people to add some peer pressure, too.

## 3.4. How Long Will It Take to Write Your Book?

How long will it take to write your book? Unfortunately, the answer to this question is about as unsatisfactory as the answer to how many words you should write each day or week. How long it takes to write your book obviously depends on how much time you spend writing.

Many people consider an author prolific if they publish one book per year or more. Unfortunately, that's not a fair comparison. For example, authors like Janet Evanovich and Nora Roberts write relatively short books. The books they write are also usually not very research-intensive. When you compare that with a book like Margaret Mitchell's "Gone with the Wind" or Tolkien's "Lord of the Rings", there is a big difference. It shouldn't come as a surprise that you can write more books when they are shorter or part of a series.

Therefore, you don't have to feel bad if it takes you several years to write your book. For example, J.K. Rowling said it took her 5 years to write the first Harry Potter book. The good news is that your second book might get finished a lot quicker than your first. However, if you want to finish your current novel before too long, you need to take the writing process seriously and make writing your novel a top priority.

The great news is that writing a book is something you can accomplish. You may need a little bit of encouragement along the way, and you'll probably get tired of doing it, but you should never give up. Writing a book can be a long process similar to trying to quit smoking or dropping some unwanted pounds. As it is, you're going to fall short of your daily or weekly goals at times, but as long as you keep picking yourself back up, you'll make it to the finish line. Similarly, you can mess up on your diet on occasion and still lose pounds as long as you don't allow one slipup to wreck your entire diet.

So how long will it take to write your book? The answer is completely up to you.

# Chapter 4:

# Get Started Writing

Now that you set up your writing area, it's time to get started with writing. Your computer is on, you have the room to yourself, and your coffee is still hot. So what should you do first? Should you brainstorm a good title? Should you come up with a good story idea? Should you outline each chapter? Should you use a name generator to come up with great names for your characters?

If you've just decided to write a book, you may not have anything to work with yet. That can work for some people. Some people can sit down at a blank screen and start writing. But most authors prefer working with a general outline of their story.

## 4.1. Should You Use an Outline?

When it comes to outlining versus writing your story, there are about as many opinions as there are writers. Many writers need at least a general outline to get started. Some writers need to plan out every little detail of their story before they commit to putting it down on paper. Then there are writers who don't enjoy outlining and abhor the entire process.

## *Advantages of Outlining*

Outlining has certain advantages. First of all, having even a broad outline helps you know where you're going with your story. It might even help relieve blank-page syndrome and give you that nudge you need to get started writing your book.

If you're working with a general outline, you'll have a basic idea of what's going to happen to your characters and your story. So you'll be writing with a sense of flow. You're not likely to get sidetracked into minor issues. Another advantage of outlining is that it can speed up your writing. If you don't have to think about what's going to happen in your story, you can just write and write and write.

And if you don't like where your story is going after all, you can always veer off the beaten path. Your outline is not there to restrict you, but rather the opposite. A good outline will give you the nudge you need to keep writing.

## *Disadvantages of Outlining*

Obviously, there are some disadvantages to outlining. For one, it may spoil the mystery of the writing process. If you already know how your story is going to end, do you still want to write it? Some authors find that knowing what's going to happen makes them less inclined to write it down. After all, they're already done with the story in their head.

Outlining may also not work well for your story. If your characters turn out differently than expected as you're writing your book, your story may not be suitable or believable. Of course, you can always change your outline if you find that it doesn't work for your story.

Finally, breaking down your story and outlining the details ahead of time may stop your creative juices from flowing. Some writers don't like to write within certain constraints. They tend to be more creative when the story has not been predetermined.

## A Little Bit Goes a Long Way

Some authors can just sit down and start writing. They may have an outline in their head; or they may create the story as they go along. But most of us need a little bit more help in the beginning. You don't have to know what's going to happen in each chapter in order to put your story down on paper. But it could help to know what your overall plot will be.

## Anarchy Can Be Good

The creative process of writing requires some anarchy. After all, your characters should develop inside of your story, and what they do may be dictated by who they are and who they become. Plus, most writers make changes to their story as they write because they end up disliking their original idea. In the end, you have to be flexible as a writer to finish a novel that's worth reading.

## *Find What Works for You*

As an author, you have to find out what works best for you. You can just start writing without any outline or general story ideas if you feel creative. Alternatively, you can try creating a general outline before you start working on your novel. In the end, you may choose to do a little bit of both.

Most writing software, including Novelize, allows you to do it either way. You can create a general plot for your story and use it to outline your novel chapter by chapter. But you can also go to the writing screen and start typing.

# *4.2. How Does Outlining Work?*

Outlining is actually quite simple. The first step is to generate a quick summary of your story. What is happening to your main characters in your book? You shouldn't focus on details but quickly jot down the overall gist of your story.

The general outline is comparable to an elevator pitch. This outline should tell a reader what's going on in your story and get them interested enough to read it. You can find examples of this on the back cover of most books.

Next, you come up with an exciting beginning. The sooner you can create a big conflict in your story, the better, mainly because it's tough to keep your reader engaged if nothing is happening in your story.

Then you need to come up with a quick summary of the middle. There could be an exciting twist in the story, the introduction of another important character, or both.

Last but not least, you need to come up with a good ending. Ideally, all of the loose ends are wrapped up in a way that makes sense for your story.

After you complete the general outline, it's time to move into chapters. You can use the snowflake method and start typing up a sentence or two about what happens in each chapter until you get to the end. Then all you have to do is write out the story.

You may also prefer to write with a general idea of your story and type along as you go. It's completely up to you. It may be helpful to plan for a few major and minor events and conflicts. You may also consider planning the appearance of several major and minor characters.

## 4.3. How Can You Come Up with a Story Idea?

The most difficult part of writing a novel may be to come up with story ideas. If you're having trouble coming up with a good story idea, there are numerous ways to find one. Every novel needs a central conflict. Fortunately, this conflict doesn't necessarily have to be a war or even a fight between individuals. The conflict could be as simple as requiring your main character to make a tough decision.

You can find story ideas from reading other books. You can get story ideas from your own life or the life of your acquaintances. You could even write about someone you knew from High School and imagined what happened to them. You can find inspiration from movies and music, too.

While I don't want to encourage you to eavesdrop on other people, you can often get excellent story ideas from the bits of conversation you happen to overhear. After all, people talk to each other everywhere. So start listening to what people are saying at the park, at the library, at the restaurant, and in line at the post office.

Watching the news can also give you story ideas. In fact, if you pay attention, you'll have a hard time not coming up with a story. The question is whether it's a good one or not.

## *4.4. Writing Prompts*

Here are a few writing prompts to get you start thinking creatively. You can take any of these story ideas and tweak them to your liking. You can even combine some of them. Even if you don't like any of these writing prompts, some of them may spark your imagination enough to come up with an even better idea for your novel.

- A soccer mom drops off her kids at school before heading out to eliminate her next target.
- 17-year-old girl is determined to find her parents even though everyone around her knows why it's a bad idea.

- Dear diary, today I shot somebody.
- A team of assassins receive a photo and have 72 ours to eliminate the target.
- A 3,000-year-old druid is forced to leave Earth for the first time and must cope with space travel.
- Even though she was severely overweight, she was invisible to her classmates. 10 years later, nobody would have recognized her. Little do they know how much misery her revenge will cause....
- She met her true love after all this time. But how can she explain that she is pregnant with a baby she can't keep?
- He thought it was just going to be another one of those days at the office. But then he looked out of the window and froze.......
- Nothing ever happened to her, but somehow people around her had a tendency to suffer from misfortunes. Until one day when she realized it was not a coincidence.......
- A new prescription is making her husband behave very strangely. His pain is gone, but the medication makes him unable to tell a lie.
- A sexy woman moves into a new house. She finds out the dreamy guy next door is a CIA agent. What's a girl to do? Spy on the spy, of course.
- After WW III leaves the planet in ruins, the remaining population takes to underwater cities to escape Mother Nature gone crazy.

- Cyber terrorists threaten to take down most of the world's governments. Can a new international team of hackers stop them before the world goes into chaos?

## 4.5 How Do You Write that First Scene?

There are many different ways to start your first scene. In the beginning, you should write whatever you feel like writing. You'll probably end up revising the first scene quite a bit since it's very important to your book.

Why is the first scene so important? If the first scene is boring, your readers will find another book to read. Think about it. How many pages are you willing to suffer through before you give up and read a different book? I don't want to put pressure on you…..just make it good.

Fortunately, there are a lot of different ways to start your book. For example, you can start the first scene by diving into the conflict. Your first scene can also be a flashback of history, or your first scene can be about your character starting another day in their life.

The most important part about the first scene is to get it written. Don't worry too much about whether it's good or gripping or full of spelling mistakes. Start writing and get your story rolling. Maybe you could find a way for the reader to identify with the character and expose a minor character flaw as soon as possible.

The only thing you should probably avoid doing in the first scene is going into a lot of background information and details that would bore your readers. Just tell them what they need to know and move the story along. You can still give them the background information later, but you can do it as the story unfolds or in condensed form along the way.

For inspiration, you may want to read the first scenes of your favorite books. How did they start? What did you like about that beginning, and how would you make it better?

# Chapter 5:

# Stop Procrastinating and Keep Writing

Procrastination is a bad word. Unfortunately, there are probably more than 1 million reasons not to write your book. After all, you have a full-time job, 4 kids (maybe you don't have 4 kids, but I do), plenty of household chores, yoga classes, yardwork, and you need sleep, too. We all lead busy lives. In fact, few people have the ability to do nothing at all even if they don't have to worry about earning a living.

The good news is that plenty of authors have already accomplished what you want to do. If they can write a book, so can you! After all, they only have 168 hours available each week just like you. Lots of people say they don't have time to do things, but the truth is that we always find the time to do the things we truly want to do.

The following chapters are here to help you overcome your excuses, work around the obstacles, and use your time effectively.

# Chapter 6:

# Do You Have Kids?

If you are a parent, you're not alone. That's the good news. The bad news is that having kids can take up a lot more time than not having kids or having pets instead. Of course there's nothing wrong with being a parent. In fact, I highly recommend it if you haven't tried it. But when you examine having kids from the perspective of time, there is no argument that a lot of it is going to be spend caring for them and being with them.

Generally, the younger your kids are, the more time they demand and need from you. Babies and toddlers usually need you to help them throughout the day and night. From changing diapers to feeding and putting them to bed, you'll basically be working 24/7.

On the other hand, older kids can often understand longer periods of absence. They may even cheer you on when you retreat into your writing corner because they are excited that you're doing what makes you happy. And since it's pretty easy for older kids to entertain themselves and give you the space you need, I'll focus the following strategies on the younger and more challenging age groups.

# 6.1. When You Have a Baby

Writing a book or getting any kind of work done when you're taking care of a baby can be extremely challenging. If you have more than one child, you may be able to take advantage of a few minutes here and there when the kids are playing together. But since you'll always want to be within earshot if not within sight, you need to be able to work wherever they are located. This means using a portable device, like a laptop or tablet or even your phone, or a paper notebook and a pen for writing.

And while you might write the occasional word or two while you're watching your little one play, the bulk of your writing time will probably be during a time when your child is asleep. Any parent of a young child will tell you how precious naptime is. The problem with using naptime for writing is that you'll have to figure out how to take care of other household chores when your baby is awake.

For a baby that isn't mobile yet, the best thing you can do is to invest in a good sling. You can carry your baby around with you when you vacuum, cook, and shovel snow. Infants love being part of the action, and you'll enjoy a much closer bond with your baby as a result. Shoveling snow is a lot more fun when you can kiss on your baby between bursts of hard work. If you're lucky, your baby may even enjoy sleeping in the sling while you're writing your book. However, don't be surprised if your baby prefers you to be moving. After all, that's what they were used to from being carried around in the womb.

Since having a young baby is exhausting even when you're not trying to write a book at the same time, it's important to cut yourself some slack. Your little one will grow up before you know it. It's much more important to savor the time you have while your child is so little and needs you around the clock than to write a book. In fact, it might be a good idea to set very low expectations for your novel writing until your baby is a little bit older.

Another thing you have to do when you're the parent of a young child is asking your partner to chip in with household chores and baby care. Whether you're a stay-at-home parent or a full-time employee, you need some time to relax. Plus, your partner should have a good amount of time to bond with your baby, too. It will help both of them.

Last but not least, when you have a young baby, you should try to let go of perfection. Your house doesn't have to be perfectly clean. After all, you're not expecting the Queen of England to visit, are you?

One of the most difficult things new mothers have to deal with is lack of sleep. While there are no miracle cures that will make your baby sleep through the night, there is something you can do to get a better night's sleep: you can try co-sleeping with your baby.

With co-sleeping, your baby may still nurse all night long, but you don't necessarily have to be awake for it. Of course, you have to follow safe co-sleeping practices to make this a viable option, but co-sleeping has numerous other benefits besides helping you get more shuteye.

I have to mention again how important it is to share the responsibility with your partner. While fathers can't breastfeed infants, they can still help with diapering and rocking the baby to sleep. It might be a good idea to talk to your partner about when they can help out. Mothers might be able to get work done during the day when their partners take the baby out for a stroll. Dads can also use an infant sling while doing other activities to give you a little bit of time to do something else.

But even with all of these tips, if your baby is still young, you probably won't get as much work done as you'd like to. Please do not feel guilty about it. Instead, you should enjoy your little one as much as you can. You can always write a novel later, but your child will never be a baby again. And while all ages of childhood are precious, young children need your love and presence the most.

## *Make Exceptions*

One of the most important rules to follow when you have a new baby is to learn to make exceptions. Today might not be the day you clean the kitchen, vacuum the living room, and write another 1,000 words, because your baby has a runny nose and is teething. Simply take it in stride. This too shall pass.

I know this book is about finding the time to write your novel, and now I keep saying you shouldn't try so hard when you have a baby. It's a little contradictive, but I think you need to keep your priorities straight. The first year is important for you and your baby, and therefore, everything else will take second place when your baby needs you 24/7.

The good news is that babies grow up. In the meantime, here is a list of concrete suggestions to start typing some words in your novel when you have a baby:

- Schedule writing time and ask your partner to be in charge of the baby.
- Don't make other plans for naptime.
- Use a sling to do household chores while your baby is up.
- Spend time outside every day with your baby to help him differentiate between day and night. Outside time is good for both of you for a lot of other reasons, too.
- Lower the bar a little bit but don't give up writing altogether (write for 3 days a week instead of 5, or write 500 words each day instead of 1,000).
- Take a day off when your baby is sick or teething (no use trying to accomplish anything) and enjoy snuggle time.
- Take good care of yourself with proper nutrition and exercise to keep your energy levels up.

- Take naps with your baby on days that you are too tired and worn out to get anything done.
- Schedule some time for other activities that allow you to recuperate and rest (such as a reading a good book or soaking in the tub).

## *Schedule Weekly Work Dates*

Everybody always tells parents how important it is to spend time with each other after the baby comes, and that's true. But it's also important to spend time doing the things you love to do and work on your own goals. For this reason, I recommend scheduling personal time for you and your partner at least once a week. Sunday morning or afternoon might be a good time to do this if it works out for both of you.

It doesn't matter when you schedule this time as long as you get (mostly) uninterrupted time to work on your book. If you're a nursing mother and have an infant, you'll need to take breaks to feed your child. But other than that, you should let your partner take care of diapering, rocking, and playing with your baby.

In an ideal situation, either you or your partner will leave the house during your working hours to reduce distractions. If that's not possible because your baby is napping, or it's too close to feeding time, you may want to lock yourself into your office or bedroom. It may take a little bit of time to get used to this and be productive, but you'll feel so much better after getting some time to work on your own project.

Of course, this personal project time should be available to both partners. It can be used for anything you want to do. If you'd rather take a nap or go out to eat with a friend, that's fine, too.

## Hire a Babysitter or Outsource Your Household Chores

Last but not least, you may want to consider hiring a babysitter on occasion to get some work done on your novel. Generally, parents hire babysitters to get a chance to go out as a couple, but babysitters are also useful on other occasions.

By now you're probably wondering how you can possibly justify the cost of a babysitter for having some time to write a novel. Think of it this way: if writing your novel gives you a happiness boost, spending money on a babysitter to do that is just as valid as paying for a babysitter to go out to eat.

Hiring a babysitter is not necessarily cheap. And good babysitters can be hard to find. How can you overcome that challenge? Here are a few suggestions:

- Ask a family member to watch your child (grandparents, aunts, uncles, or godparents).
- Hire a mother's helper, a tween or young teen, who will watch your child and play with her while you're still in the house writing your book.
- Trade babysitting services with another family.

Working parents often pay for daycare or a nanny to watch their children during working hours anyway. You might be able to extend those hours a little bit to get some work done before you pick up your child. If you're not comfortable with letting someone else watch your baby during that first year, you'll have to rely on your partner to give you a break.

Alternatively, you might decide to hire someone to do your household chores instead of babysitting so that you can utilize naptimes and bedtimes for bigger and better things. Here are a few suggestions for chores to outsource:

- Mowing the lawn
- Cleaning bathrooms
- Doing laundry
- Washing cloth diapers
- Grocery shopping
- Shoveling snow
- Cooking

It pays to be creative. If you find yourself spending a lot of time doing activities that aren't fun, you may want to consider reducing the time you spend on them. When it comes to cooking and kitchen cleanup, you can start cooking in batches, making simpler meals, buying prepackaged dinners, going out to eat, or ordering food.

You could also choose to trade certain chores with your neighbors. This might be less common but just as effective in the long run. For example, in return for mowing their lawn, they might supply you with a few dinners each week.

For many families, it's easier to reduce the number of household chores or the time you spend doing them than to outsource. For example, while you have to mow your lawn, do you have to mow it every week? You have to do laundry, but does it need to be done every day? Batching grocery trips, cleaning and tidying, and cooking chores can drastically reduce the amount of time you spend on household tasks every week. This is great, since our goal is to free up some time for you to write your book.

## 6.2. When You Have a Preschooler

Having a preschooler is easier than having a baby or a toddler. After all, they start learning how to do a lot of things on their own, including dressing themselves, helping you around the house with setting the table and occasionally cleaning up, and going to the bathroom. But even though preschoolers are more capable of doing things without you, that doesn't mean they require less attention than a baby or toddler.

### You Have to Spend Time Outside

In order to keep your preschooler happy, it's important to meet their needs. If you try to get work done in the morning, they will whine and nag all day long asking you to play with them. It's much better to take them to the playground, the park, the zoo, or wherever you like to go in the morning and allow them to run around and play. After that, they're much more likely to want to sit in their room or in the playroom and play quietly with toys while you can get some things done around the house or write your book.

Outside playtime should be on your schedule every day. Going outside is the best thing you can do with a young child, and it doesn't even cost anything. Of course it's important to dress appropriately for the weather, but you probably remember how much fun it was for you to jump in puddles or dance in the rain as a child, don't you?

Here is something I've learned after having four kids of my own: when kids make a mess, it's never as bad as you think it will be. I even let my kids play in the mud outside while wearing their bathing suits and cleaned them up afterwards. Of course we live in Texas, which means the outside temperature was warm enough for them to do that. But I also didn't stop my 2-year-old from painting with finger paint or acrylic paint with his big sisters because I know that I can wash it off afterwards. For some reason having fun often involves getting messy.

## Don't Abuse the TV as a Babysitter

Every parent has done this. If you want your kids to be quiet and leave you alone for a little while, you either have to feed them (the unhealthier the food, the longer they stay quiet) or stick them in front of the TV. But while it sounds like a great babysitter, the TV really isn't. On that note, feeding your kids junk food isn't a good idea, either, but you already know that.

At our house, we schedule movie days. On those days, one of the kids gets to pick which movie they want to watch. After that, we turn the TV off. The only time when my kids get to sit in front of the TV all day is when they go to Grandma's house. Why is limiting TV so important? Here are several reasons I can think of:

- Your kids will keep whining for more if you don't set a limit.
- Your kids will ask you to buy everything they see during commercials.

- Your kids will lose the ability to use their imagination.
- Watching too much TV will harm your child's vision.
- Your child will miss out on playtime.

There is nothing wrong with breaking the rules on occasion. In fact, watching a funny movie together can be a great way to get through a rainy day without a play date. But relying on the TV to keep your child entertained throughout the day is not going to teach them to use their imagination and entertain themselves.

## Let Them Help You

Preschoolers love to help. This is the age where your child wants to do everything you're doing, whether it's sweeping, cleaning the table, baking, doing laundry, planting flowers, or cleaning out the cat litter box. If at all possible, you should let your child help you. Of course they're not going to do the tasks as well as you can do them on your own, and certainly not as fast as you can do them without their help, but that's not a good enough reason to exclude them.

Letting your children help you now will make it more likely they'll continue pitching in with household chores in the future. Pretending to be Mommy or Daddy is also a great way for your kids to learn new skills. How do you think they learned everything else they know how to do? Kids are great imitators, and that's why they know how to walk and talk without having had any formal lessons for either skill.

One thing your child can't help you with is writing a novel. However, you can give them an old keyboard of their own so they can pretend to be writing. Our kids love "working" on their keyboard like their parents.

## Get Your Partner Involved

Whether you're a stay-at-home parent or work full-time, your partner has to pitch in with childcare. The person who takes care of the kids most of the time usually knows best how to entertain them, get them to do certain activities, and generally keep them occupied. In my family that happens to be me.

But because I know how to play with the kids and keep them happy doesn't mean my husband can't do the same. When I want to work, I ask him to take care of the kids. However, I learned that I can't ask him to watch them because inevitably they come and find me, at least the little ones do. So here is what we've had to do:

I tell my older girls that they need to ask their Dad if they need anything because I want to get some work done. I ask my husband to do something specific with the younger crew, for example I will suggest that he reads a few books with them. You can also ask your partner to take the kids to the backyard or to the park in order to give you some quiet time. Letting you have the house to yourself can be especially helpful if your computer is sitting in the middle of the kids' play area.

You could also combine two things in one by asking your partner to take the kids grocery shopping. My husband always does the grocery shopping, and he doesn't mind taking the kids (yes, he's even taken all four of them on occasion).

## *Plan Strategically*

When you have preschoolers, you have to plan a little bit. Parents are fine with staying home and doing nothing, but preschoolers are constantly on the go. They're like wind-up toys that never run out of batteries or like the energizer bunny that just keeps going and going and going... In order to get the most out of your day and keep your sanity, you need to plan strategically.

If you know your child is more likely to be clingy and whiny in the evening, then that's not a good time to try to write. Of course as a parent you'll probably get used to writing with lots of interruptions. But ideally, you should work when your child can find other things to occupy their time with.

There are different ways to keep kids occupied and keep them out of trouble. Here are a few suggestions:

• Let them eat a snack in the living room and pretend it's a picnic.
• Get out a few special toys that they can only play with when you're working. They might even start encouraging you to work to play with those toys.
• Invite your child to play dress up.

- Ask your child to build you a tall tower out of blocks or Duplos.
- Give your child an art project, e.g. making a necklace out of beads, playing with Play-Doh, drawing a picture with crayons, or making a collage with stickers.
- Ask your child to take the stuffed animals to the vet and make them feel better.

One thing I do not recommend: letting your kids play with water unsupervised. I let my son play with soapy water in the sink for a while because he enjoyed playing with the bubbles. In my case, that led to the drowning of a library book that was left on the bathroom floor and consequently cost me $10. In hindsight, that wasn't really worth the few minutes it gave me to work on something else.

## Work When They're Sleeping

The best time to get work done is when your child is sleeping. Fortunately, most children need more sleep than adults. Maybe nature designed it this way to help us cope with the task of parenting and avoid burnout. Plus, if your child didn't sleep while you were awake, you'd never get a chance to do all the things you can't do when your child is around. For example, you could eat chocolate without having to share, or you could practice making babies with your partner.

Needless to say, bedtime is something we tend to look forward to at my house (minus the actual part of putting the kids to bed). During the evening, we can do the things we want to do without worrying about the short people we choose to share our lives with.

I used to be a big advocate of early bedtimes. When my girls were younger, they would be in bed by 6 p.m. They also got up early at 6 a.m. Back then, I was always flabbergasted when I saw young children at the grocery store at 10 p.m.

While I still like early bedtimes, my boys won't go to bed as early as that. Maybe it has something to do with the fact that we embraced co-sleeping. Maybe it's just how they're wired. But we're happy when they're asleep by 10 p.m. On the plus side, they also sleep in a little later, although not as late as I'd like them to. One of them is still sleeping in our bed with us, so there is a chance that he'll go to bed earlier once he moves into a room with his siblings. In the meantime, we have to make do with what we've got.

If you have trouble getting your kids to sleep earlier, you may try slowly moving their bedtime. If you do it in small increments, it makes it easier for them to adjust. You still want to make sure they're getting enough sleep for the day and not waking up sooner than they should. You can try adjusting bedtime in 15-minute increments and wait a week before moving it up again.

When it comes to shuteye, every child and adult is a little different. Some kids don't need as much sleep as other kids. But if they're constantly fussy or hungry, they might benefit from going to bed earlier.

# 6.3. When You Have a School-age Child

When your kids are old enough to go to school, they are generally old enough to understand what it means when you have to work. Unfortunately, that doesn't always stop them from bothering you while you're in the middle of writing an exciting chapter. The good news is that there are some things you can do to keep them occupied and away from your computer without turning on the TV.

## Work Alongside Them

Your kids may not be writing a novel, but they probably have to do homework on a regular basis. What's better than working on your novel while they write an essay for school or work on their math problems?

If you own a laptop or tablet, you can sit at the same table with them. This way you're still around to help them when they need you, but you're also making progress on your book. If your kids get to see you work, then they might feel more motivated to do their own work, too. At the very least, you'll be setting a good example for them.

## Take Advantage of Playdates

Kids love to play. That's a given. And whether you have one or more children, there will probably be a large number of playdates with friends over the years.

While your kids are having fun at a friend's house, you should be working on your novel. The laundry and the dishes can wait. Similarly, if the playdate is happening at your house, you can work on your novel while the kids play together. After all, they don't need you, do they?

Working on your novel while they're playing also gives you the ability to spend time with them when they're done. It helps you avoid having to spread your focus. After all, you can be much more relaxed after you have met your word count goal for the day.

## Make Sporting Events Count

Many children are signed up for extracurricular activities. Whether your kids play soccer, football, or T-ball, or whether they dance, do gymnastics, or practice ballet, you can expect to spend a lot of time on the sidelines.

It's a lot of fun to watch your kids practice and perform, but that doesn't mean your eyes have to be glued onto your child at all times. In fact, you probably already spend most of the time talking to other Moms or reading books. The next time you have to sit around at a game or performance, you should take your laptop with you and work on your novel instead.

## Enlist Their Cooperation

School-age kids know what it's like to have deadlines. After all, they have to do homework almost every day. If you want to write your novel, it might be a good idea to talk to your kids about it.

If appropriate, you could tell them what your story is all about. You could also ask them if they can help you get your book written by giving you time to write. They'll probably be pretty reasonable about it.

# Chapter 7:

# Do You Have a Job or Two?

Most people have to work full-time in order to pay their bills. Having a job can create a bit of a vicious cycle. While you need to go to work every day, you may find that you never have time to work on your novel or on any other projects. But if you never write and publish books, you'll never make a living as a writer allowing you to quit working.

It looks like a catch 22, but you might feel better when you realize that many published authors have other jobs, except for the ones that make a really good living with writing.

The good news is that you can go to work and still work on your book in your free time. Yes, you have free time even if you currently don't think you do. After all, you have 24 hours every day just like every other human being on the planet.

# 7.1. Don't Agree to Work Overtime

Before we get into it any further, I want to address the issue of working too much. Some people truly work too much. It's not unusual for many people to work 60 hours or more. That's not a problem if this only happens for a limited period of time. For example, an accountant may work a lot of hours during tax season. But working overtime should not be a normal way of life for you.

If you always work overtime at your job, you have two options to reduce your hours. You can talk to your boss and let them know that you're not willing to continue working overtime. You can be nice about it, but you have to let them know that working overtime on a regular basis is interfering with your personal and family time. Technically, you don't have to give a reason for not working overtime, but people tend to expect one whenever you say no to them.

If your employer is used to you working overtime, you may need to help them figure out how to cut down your hours. For example, you can suggest reducing your workload to make it possible, whether that means hiring additional staff or getting rid of superfluous activities. If your boss is receptive, that's great. However, you should start cutting down your hours soon, or your boss won't think you meant it.

If your employer isn't thrilled about your suggestions, you're going to have to go with another option to get rid of overtime: find another job. When it comes to working overtime, it's not just the fact that you don't have time to write your novel or have some resemblance of a personal life. The thing is that working overtime adversely affects your productivity, because most people are less productive the longer they work. Basically, working 10-hour days doesn't necessarily mean increased productivity compared to working for 8 hours.

What if you have to work overtime in order to pay the bills? Again, you have more than one option. You can ask for a raise and gradually reduce your hours. You can find a different job or become self-employed.

## 7.2. Take Control of Your Life

Let's assume you have to work overtime, and there is nothing you can do to change that. However, I'm still of the opinion that people are more in charge of their lives they ever were before; and the only thing that's stopping you from doing what you want to do is you. Nevertheless, there may be special circumstances that lead you to choose working overtime at this particular time in your life. What if you want to keep working the same hours and still write a novel?

It's possible. However, you'll probably have to reduce the time you spend doing other things in order to make it work. You may get up earlier in the morning to get some writing done. You may forego relaxing and talking to your colleagues during your lunchbreak and work on your novel instead. You may have to cancel your cable TV and spend time writing in the evening.

The thing is even though you have a whopping 24 hours you can use to accomplish something each day, time is still limited. If you're doing one thing, then you can't be doing another thing. And yes, some things can be done simultaneously, such as eating and watching TV or running on the treadmill and watching TV, but writing isn't one of those activities.

In the end, it all comes down to choice. Do you choose to spend some of your precious time to work on your novel, or would you rather use the "I'm too busy at work" excuse to keep writing a novel a dream for you? If you chose the first option, keep reading, because I'll tell you how to do it.

# Chapter 8:

# Are You In Charge of the Household?

Whether you're in charge of running the household or helping out with chores on occasion doesn't change the fact that laundry, doing dishes and cleaning are repetitive, thankless tasks that probably take up a lot of your time. The good news is that there are many ways to reduce the time you spend on doing household chores without anyone being the worse off for it. However, in order to do this, you may have to cultivate a better understanding of the word "clean" and let go of wanting everything to be perfect.

## 8.1. How Clean Does Your House Really Need to Be?

Before we talk about how to clean your house effectively and let others help you get the job done, it's important to figure out how clean your house needs to be. Everybody has a different comfort level when it comes to messiness. Some people cannot go to bed with dirty dishes sitting in the sink. Others only draw the line when the roaches start appearing.

I'm not suggesting that you let your house get so bad that nobody will ever want to come over again. That's obviously not a good way to live. However, I do think that many people spend too much time on cleaning and not enough time on doing other, more productive and more exciting tasks.

It's a good idea to write down what you want your home to look like. For example, would you like the dishes to be put away every night, the beds made in the morning, and your desk cleaned off every day? Does it bother you when the kids leave their toys in the living room? If so, how much does it bother you? How often do you want to vacuum the carpet and clean the bathrooms?

Once you figure out what you want done in terms of housekeeping, it's time to come up with a cleaning schedule. A cleaning schedule may sound annoying, but it will free you from having to clean constantly. When you notice that the bathroom needs to be cleaned, you don't have to drop everything and do it. The same is true for doing laundry. Anything that has to get done in the household will get done because you already have it scheduled on the calendar. This frees you in the moment to do something else.

## Schedule Your Household Tasks

Before you put any of your household tasks on a schedule, you should figure out whether you could eliminate them first. For example, do you need to mop underneath your fridge? Nobody ever checks under there anyways….

At the very least, you should reduce the frequency of performing the task to the bare minimum. For example, if you have enough clothes to last you through the week, you don't need to do laundry more often than every 7 days. The longer you can stretch it out, the less time you spend on the task.

So here is what you need to do next. Get out whatever you use to schedule meetings, appointments, and other activities, whether that's a traditional wall calendar, a small notebook, or your cell phone. Now schedule the tasks you want done. In order to save the most amount of time, you should bunch all of your cleaning tasks into one time slot. For example, Saturday morning could be your clean-up-the-house time. And this event should be all-hands-on-deck to get it done as quickly as possible. One person can pick up toys, someone else can sweep while the next person cleans the bathroom. Yes, I'm telling you to make your kids help. After all, they cause some or most of the mess, don't they?

If your house is really big and there are a lot of chores to do, you may need to split them up over 2 or 3 evenings. But remember, the less time you spend on cleaning, the more time you have for other things.

## *Split the Workload*

The great thing about household tasks is that most people hate doing them all equally. Therefore, it's not fair for one person to do everything. Instead, you should split the workload.

If you have kids, you're probably still going to want to make it fair by rotating every task evenly among your family members. This means everyone will get every chore at some point. They may even be less inclined to make a mess because they know they'll have to clean it up later (but don't expect miracles).

You could get out a few Popsicle sticks, write the chores that need to be done on each of them, and have everyone pull the same number of sticks. This prevents people from always doing the same chores and helps your kids learn how to do it all (so eventually, you don't have to). It also turns cleaning into a game and might even make it a little bit more fun, especially since everybody "loses" and has to do something.

## Require Everyone to Clean Up after Themselves

Having to clean the kitchen wouldn't be so daunting if everyone got into the habit of cleaning up after themselves. Even young children can learn to put their dishes and silverware in the sink and help set the table for dinner. But the older your children get, the more important it is to encourage them to clean up after themselves.

Of course the same is true for your partner or roommate. It's fine to leave dirty socks on the floor occasionally, but you shouldn't feel obligated to pick up after them. You don't have to police anyone, either. If your kids (or partner) keep forgetting to put stuff away, then you should leave it there for them to do later. Eventually, they'll get it. At least that's the hope.

## *Play Beat the Clock*

One of the most effective ways to clean is to play "beat the clock" while you're doing it. Do you know that the more time you have to complete a task, the longer it takes? If you have 8 hours to complete a project at work, you're not going to get it done in 5 or 3 hours. After all, you were given all this time to do it. On the other hand, when you have to leave work early, you usually scramble around and get all of your ducks in a row in a lot shorter amount of time than it normally takes you to do the same tasks.

It's no different with cleaning. If you plan to clean and do laundry all weekend, then that's what you'll be doing all weekend. Who wants to do that? Instead, schedule 2 or 3 hours at the most to do a round of basic cleanup. It probably won't be perfect, but there should be some significant improvement when you're done.

## *What to Clean to Make a Difference*

When cleaning time is limited, it's important to clean the right things to make a difference. What gives you the biggest bang for your buck? It turns out cleaning flat surfaces and eliminating random clutter does more for your room than picking up every single toy on the floor. So next time you want to make the house look nice, attack the countertops in your kitchen, bathrooms, living room, and any other flat surface you find.

## *Consider Outsourcing Your Household Chores*

I used to think that only rich people could afford to hire a cleaning service. But that's not entirely true. If you think about it, even a middle-income family probably earns more money per hour than the cleaning service that comes and cleans your home. Therefore, it doesn't make a lot of sense for them to spend their valuable time cleaning when they could be working and making money instead.

I personally do not have a cleaning service, and I have never used one. However, that doesn't mean you can't. If you want to get rid of some of the pesky household chores without going broke, you might consider paying for the chores you hate doing the most. For example, you can ask them to clean the bathroom.

If you end up cleaning your house all day before the cleaning service arrives because you're embarrassed about the mess in your home, maybe outsourcing your household chores won't work for you. However, you can outsource them to the short people who are living in your home with you. Even elementary-school age kids are old enough to do some basic household chores. And they're usually a lot cheaper than a cleaning service, too. You may have to show them what you want them to do a few times, but it definitely pays off in free time for you later.

Of course there are a lot of different opinions on whether you should pay kids to do chores. Personally, I expect them to help out in the household as being part of our family. But when I was little, part of my allowance was tied to cleaning the bathroom on a weekly basis, which worked well for both me and my parents.

# Chapter 9:

# Don't Let Your Doubts Hold You Back

Maybe the reason you haven't written a novel yet is that you don't think you'll be any good as an author. If you have doubts about your ability as a writer, you're certainly not alone. It's quite understandable to postpone writing a book forever. After all, if you don't write it, nobody will find out that you're not any good at writing.

Of course it's much better if you look at it from a different perspective. If you've never written more than a few mandatory essays in school, it's quite possible that your writing is far from perfect. The good news is that that's not a problem. As you work on your craft, your writing will get better overtime. The more you write, the sooner you'll figure out what type of story you can tell well.

If it makes you feel better, even some famous authors are embarrassed with some of their early works. For example, Janet Evanovich stated that her first novels were not good at all. She said she wrote in the perspective of the guy in her romance novels, and the results were not good. She actually didn't get a publishing contract until she sent out her third novel.

It's easy for me to tell you to try it out and get better. But you probably don't want to hear that your first novel might not make the New York Times Bestseller List. Then again it just might. How do you know if you don't try?

The great thing is that you don't have to put your writing out there for the world to see without getting some feedback from a few individuals first. Your friends and family members are probably not the best people to ask to be Beta readers since they won't want to hurt your feelings. Instead, you might like to take excerpts of your writing to a local writing group for useful suggestions.

Do you still doubt that you can write a good novel worth reading? Let me give it another try. You're not ready to give up on your dreams so quickly, are you? I didn't think so!

In order to find the courage to do something new, you might have to remember another time when you had to go out of your comfort zone. Maybe it was the time you went on a blind date, or the time you asked your boss for a promotion and a raise, or the time when you realized you could stand up for what you want. Life offers a lot of opportunities to prove to yourself that you can succeed at doing something different or learning something new.

Here is what we're going to do to cross this hurtle: write down 3 things you've done that you're immensely proud of right now. Don't continue reading. Write them down right now!

1.

...........................................................................

...........................................................................

...........................................................................

2.

...........................................................................

...........................................................................

...........................................................................

3.

...........................................................................

...........................................................................

...........................................................................

Now if you can do that, you can write a novel, too! All you need is a little determination and a few of the following 24 strategies to help keep you on track.

# Chapter 10:

# 24 Strategies to Keep You Writing

Finding time to write is not easy, but it's definitely doable if you really want to do it. After all, you lead a busy life, and who doesn't? Sometimes you just have to trick yourself into doing the things you want to do instead of letting other circumstances control your life. You still have to go to work, and you still have to prepare dinner and help the kids with homework, but you can exert quite a bit of control over the rest of your time.

The following pages are dedicated to the different strategies you can implement to keep writing. Some strategies will work well together for you, but others may not apply to you. You can read through all of the following suggestions and pick the ones you think would work best. But here is the key: you have to give them a fair trial.

Most new habits take at least 30 days to take hold. During the first day or two, you probably won't have any trouble meeting your writing goals. But by the 3$^{rd}$ or 4$^{th}$ day, you'll probably come up with an excuse **not** to write. Don't fall into the trap! It's important to keep writing consistently every day, rain or shine.

After all, what you want is to build a sustainable writing habit that you can keep up for a long time. In fact, you want to keep writing until you finish that first novel. And by that time, you won't be able to stop yourself from writing another one.

You have to give each strategy a legitimate try, at least 2 or 3 weeks but preferably the full 30 days, before dismissing it as useless for you. And if you chose a strategy that doesn't work for you, then you need to try something else. Most people already know what would make a difference in their lives if they think about it hard enough.

For example, if you like to check your email every time you get on the computer and consequently spend 2 hours replying and surfing the Internet, you'll have to build a habit of checking your email only at designated times of the day instead. You may even put a time limit on email correspondence. When the timer beeps, you have to stop. You could also use rewards for not checking your email. If you turn on your computer and start writing without opening Outlook or Gmail, you can eat a cookie when you're done (or a grape if you're on a diet).

# 1. Set a Designated Time

It seems so simple, but saving yourself a spot in your calendar for getting some designated writing time might be all the motivation you need to do it. It doesn't matter what type of calendar you use as long as you keep a slot available for yourself.

Most people make the mistake of planning every required activity, such as doctor's appointments, work meetings, and your kid's soccer practice, but they don't schedule the activities that are most meaningful to them. When it comes down to it, you should give yourself first priority on your calendar. Before you add any other appointments, you should save yourself some time to exercise, time to write, and time to do whatever sounds like fun to you.

Of course you can still be flexible. Obviously, you can change your appointment with yourself if you absolutely need to, but you shouldn't make that a habit. After all, you wouldn't postpone your child's dentist appointment unless it was absolutely necessary, right? And personal time to take care of your needs is just as important as those appointments for your kids.

If there is a conflict in your schedule, the most difficult part about scheduling time to write is to take it seriously. You don't have to tell other people why you're not available at that time if that embarrasses you. You can say you already have plans and find a different time that works for both of you.

Ideally, the scheduled writing times should be one of your more productive times. If you're an early morning person, you might not want to schedule time to write in the evening. On the other hand, if you have young kids, you might need to be more flexible and try to work around nap times.

When you schedule time to write, there's no need to set it up for the same time every day, either. For example, you might be able to schedule a larger chunk of time on the weekend when you don't have work or fulfill other pressing obligations.

It doesn't matter if you only have small chunks of time available in your schedule when it comes to writing a novel, although it might be nice to enjoy a few uninterrupted hours of writing. Even having one hour set aside to work on your novel can accomplish quite a bit. The important thing is for you to schedule time regularly and as often as possible.

In fact, if you have 30 minutes every other day, that's probably more helpful for getting that novel written than having 3 consecutive hours only once a week. After all, what if you can't get over your writer's block on your writing day or miss out that day due to an important appointment? Then you have to wait an entire week to get a few more words typed up…

On the other hand, if the muse strikes you during one of your 30-minute sessions, you might be tempted to blow off meeting your coworkers for drinks later. The great thing about being a writer is that you can easily explain how you lost track of time.

It can take some time to get used to scheduling time to write. Don't feel bad if you end up staring at the screen the first few times you sit down with the intention of working on your novel. That's normal, especially if you have never worked this way in the past. But once you get into the habit of writing, the words will start to flow. And if you're still at a loss for words, use one of the writing prompts from one of the earlier chapters to get started. You don't have to write a full novel with it if you don't want to, but at least you'll get started with writing something.

## *2. Set a Minimum Word Requirement*

Setting a minimum word requirement may seem a little restrictive to you as a writer. After all, you're creative, and you want quality over quantity, right? Even so, having a goal in mind before you sit down to write can encourage you to keep going. After all, you need to have some way to measure your progress. In the book world, it's all about the number of words you've written.

The good news is that your novel may not need 100,000 words. In fact, most new novels are significantly shorter than that. But you still have to write tens of thousands of words. So the more words you write today, the closer you get to the end of your story.

There are at least two approaches to setting a minimum word count goal. Your first option is to calculate how many words you need to write each day or week in order to get your novel done by a certain date. You'll have to use an estimated total word count (even though your novel may end up being longer or shorter than you originally planned) to derive at this number.

Formula: Total word count goal divided by number of days = words per day

Example: 60,000 words / 90 days = 667 words per day

For example, if you want to write a 60,000-word novel in the next 90 days, you'll have to write 667 words per day. If you want to take off at least one day per week, you'll have to write closer to 780 words each day. Just play around with the numbers. It's okay if you're not sure how many words your novel should have or when you want to be done. Pick a number and a date and go with it.

Using this approach gives you a good indication how you're progressing with your writing, and it keeps you on track. If you fall behind, you can play catch-up by writing significantly more words each day.

Another option is to set a fairly low minimum daily word count goal that is easy for you to reach. A good example would be 500 words per day. For example, this chapter has 561 words including the heading. If you don't write 500 words one day, you could roll that over to the next day. I know of a writer who uses this approach but has a rule not to roll over any word count goals to the next month. That means, at the end of the month he's busy playing catch-up. But so far he has always met his minimum.

If you go with the minimum word count goal, you may want to set the minimum low, especially if you plan on writing every day. If you only write 2 days a week, you'll want the minimum to be higher. Otherwise, you'll take forever to get that novel done.

However, the most important aspect of setting the minimum is to get you going. Even writing 200 words a day will get a novel written eventually as long as you keep doing it. So start low and go up if you can. And if 200 words a day is the best you can do, you still don't need to feel bad. It's quite an accomplishment, especially compared to not doing anything at all.

## 3. Build a Habit

In order to be a successful writer, you have to get into the habit of writing. There is no way around this step. The good news is that once you've established your writing habit, it will be difficult for you not to write. The bad news is that we are all driven by our habits.

You may want to do things differently, but in moments of stress and uncertainty, we all fall back to doing what we have always done. Fortunately, you can change your habits. You can form new habits and get rid of old habits. This is not going to be easy, but it's possible.

By the way, examining your habits might be a good way to change other aspects of your life that you're not completely satisfied with, whether that's your career, your weight, or how you spend your free time.

In order to establish a new habit, you need to keep it up religiously for at least 30 days. The first few days of sitting down to write will probably be quite easy. You'll be wondering what's been stopping you from doing it for so long. However, at some point, you'll hit a wall.

Either you'll have a very stressful day at work, stare at the screen without knowing how to get ahead in your story, or you are so overwhelmed that you can't find a way out of those feelings. But no matter how you feel that day, you should sit down to write, even if you spend your allotted time starting at the screen. This is not the time to do the dishes instead or surf the Internet. Otherwise, you might fall off the wagon altogether.

If you absolutely can't think of anything to write to continue your story, you might want to brainstorm character names and locations. Alternatively, you could come up with an idea for a new story to work on later. While I want you to be disciplined about writing your novel, it's more important to establish your new habit of writing during that first month, even at the risk of spreading your focus a little bit.

You could also write nonsense. Sometimes the physical act of writing will overcome writer's block. And writing nonsense can be very enjoyable, especially if you paste it into an email and send it to your spouse, your coworker, or even your boss, if he or she has a sense of humor.

During that first month, you might need to resort to using rewards for meeting your writing goal to help you build the habit of writing. You should also be prepared to exercise your willpower considerably during that time.

To make it easier to write, you should pick a good time to do it. For example, you could start early in the morning before you get bogged down by work or requests from your kids if possible.

## *Start Small*

In order to make your writing habit stick, you should start out small. If you ultimately want to write for an hour every day, start with 20 minutes. You'll probably find it easier to fit in 20 minutes of writing, because it's a much smaller chunk of time. Eventually, you can increase the time until you've reached your original goal, but for now finding 20 minutes of writing time is so much better than not writing at all.

It can be hard to fall into the trap of thinking a little bit of writing isn't a great accomplishment. But you should never look at it that way because you're building a habit. If after the first 30 days, you automatically sit down to write each day without having to talk yourself into doing it, you have accomplished what many wanna-be-authors haven't. You deserve a pat on the back!

## *Never Miss Twice*

In order to build a lasting habit of any kind, you should forgive yourself when you mess up. If you eat a tub of ice cream during your diet, skip the gym on Monday, or don't sit down to write one day, then you need to pick yourself back up and get back on track the next day. It's okay not to write one day, but in order to build a lasting habit of writing you should never skip writing two days in a row.

If you didn't write anything the day before, you should get your writing done first thing in the morning if you can. You don't have to write enough to make up for the lost day, because that would probably overwhelm you at this point, leaving you to abandon writing altogether. Remember, we're still trying to build a habit here, so it's okay to start small as long as you keep going and do a little bit each day. Consistency is the most important aspect of building a habit.

## Set a Reminder

In order to build a new habit, you may need a reminder to help you. In the beginning, you might need to set an alarm in your phone to alert you. This is necessary whether you decide to write first thing in the morning or during your lunch break. Otherwise, you'll use the time to do something else not quite as productive.

Hopefully at some point, you might not need a scheduled reminder anymore. But instead of writing at a specific time each day, you could also schedule writing time after something else happens. This is called daisy-chaining your new habit onto an old one.

## Daisy-Chain a New Habit

A lot of the things we do habitually happen because of something else. For example, you probably always get dressed after you take a shower. It's logical because it's the next step. You can use this idea to help you write, too.

Every habit is preceded by a cue or reminder. Since you're already a creature of habit whether you realize it or not, you can take advantage of the habits you already have. For example, you can start writing as soon as you drink your first cup of coffee every morning, or you can work on your book after you get the mail each day. Your habit of getting the mail or drinking coffee is already firmly in place, and you're merely adding onto it.

Daisy-chaining a new habit will still require you to keep at it consistently for the next 30 days in order for it to stick, but it might not require quite as much willpower as starting a new habit on its own. That's because you're taking advantage of the things you're already doing every day. And potentially you're combining something pleasurable (drinking coffee) with something you want to do (write your book).

## *4. Find Your Most Productive Time*

Do you remember the last time it took you twice as long to accomplish a certain task because you weren't feeling very productive? Why is it that we can sometimes finish a project in 30 minutes, and other times it takes us 2 hours or more?

The big difference in people's productivity levels throughout the day and week is well documented across all industries. And we experience this gap because we all try to get things done all day long regardless of whether or not we're actually up to doing them. Partly, that's because you're at work and getting paid to look busy. But our culture also doesn't value taking an extended break in the middle of the day and returning to work with vigor after the siesta is over.

What does that mean for your novel writing? While you don't always have control over your busy schedule, you should try to schedule your writing time when you're normally most productive. For a lot of people that time is during the early morning hours. Most of us are worn out by midday and get another small burst of energy towards the end of the day.

But don't let other people's preference dictate what your most productive hours are. If you're a night owl and frequently find yourself cranking out hundreds of words after everyone else has gone to sleep, that may be the best time to write for you.

If you're not sure when you're most productive, you should experiment with different times of the day. If you don't want to go by how productive you felt, you should record the number of words you've written each time and how long that took you. Obviously, this is going to vary a little each day. But if you write twice as many words in an hour, you can save yourself some time and get your novel written faster. And you can do this just by picking a different time of day to write!

# 5. Use Reward (or Punishment)

Using rewards to encourage good behavior and discourage bad behavior is a concept that you're probably already familiar with. Whether you believe in this approach to instill discipline in your children is one thing, but you can certainly give it a try to help you build a lifelong habit of writing.

The thing about rewards and punishments is that they don't need to be severe. In fact, a lot of times you can let nature take its course, and that's often punishment enough. For example, if you have a habit of showing up late, you probably won't be able to keep your job for very long. Consequently, you may try really hard to get to work on time.

That being said, there won't be a lot of natural consequences for not writing your novel. The only thing is that you will never see your name in print. For most people that's sad but not so devastating that it will make them drop what they're doing and start writing. That's why you may have to trick yourself into writing and use rewards or punishments to keep you going.

Most people are more motivated when there is a potential for gain. This means rewards will probably work better for you than punishment. For example, after you finish writing your 500 words for the day, you get to watch an episode of your favorite TV show. You can add milestone rewards for when you've completed a big chunk of your book, too. For example, you can treat yourself by going to the spa or buying a new outfit for finishing the first half of your book. And maybe you can splurge on a new laptop when you finish the first draft of your novel.

## Make it Visible

Working hard to get a reward can be motivating, but only if you can make the reward visible. In order to do that you have to track your progress and also keep your reward within eyesight. It could be a picture of what you want that's hanging up next to your desk. For example, you could print a picture of a new outfit you might buy yourself or hang up a voucher for a spa visit. Every time you start working on your book, you'll see the reward that's waiting for you when you get done.

Another way to make it feel real is to keep track of your progress underneath your prize. When you're done for the day you can write down your updated total word count underneath the picture of the reward. It may take some time to get to the finish line, but you're getting visibly closer every day.

## *Make It Meaningful*

Setting a reward is pretty easy to do. But if you want to be motivated enough to achieve your goals and write your novel, you have to make the reward meaningful. It has to be something special you don't normally do for yourself. It has to excite you. What's exciting for you is not the same thing that would be exciting for your partner or your friend. Therefore, only you know what type of reward you should choose.

Here are some ideas for possible rewards for completing the first draft of your novel:

- Go to a concert
- Get pampered at a spa for an entire weekend
- Buy yourself a new electronic toy you've been wanting (the latest iSomething, a new laptop, a tablet, or whatever makes your heart skip a beat)
- Buy yourself a really expensive new outfit
- Splurge on hiring a babysitter for an entire weekend so you can do nothing at all
- Book a vacation to a place you've always wanted to visit

Your reward doesn't have to be big or expensive to have meaning for you. A good reward for me would be purchasing German chocolate from an online grocery store. Of course I'd love to fly to Germany to buy the chocolate in person, but that's a little out of my price range as a spur-of-the-moment adventure.

## *Find Yourself a Judge*

It's much easier to stick to your goals if you're not in charge of rewarding yourself afterwards. Let's say that you've already made plans to see your favorite group in concert as long as you finish the first draft of your book by a certain date. Now it's easy for you to cheat and go to the concert anyway. The problem is that your subconscious knows that, too, so you may find it difficult to convince yourself that you really have to write the novel in order to be able to go.

This is where getting yourself a judge comes in handy. You'll have to share your goals with someone else, such as your partner, your Mom, or your best friend. That person will get to decide if and when you deserve to get the reward you want.

Now here is the tricky part: you have to find a judge who will keep you honest. You should find someone who is good about making and sticking to commitments and ask them to help you. If you know that they're not going to be a stickler for rules and allow you to go to the concert even if you don't meet your goal, you haven't found the right judge. By the way in the concert example, you should buy tickets and give them to your judge to keep for you. If you finish your novel in time, you can get those tickets and go. If not, then you already know who'll be having fun instead of you that night.

# 6. Participate in NaNoWriMo

You may have heard of National Novel Writing Month, short NaNoWriMo. NaNoWriMo challenges you to write 50,000 words in the month of November. You're allowed to outline your novel before that, but you can't write your novel ahead of time. Other than that, there are no requirements to join NaNoWriMo. It doesn't cost any money, and you can get support from other fellow writers along the way.

In order to succeed during NaNoWriMo, you need to understand that this is only supposed to be the beginning of your first draft. 50,000 words is a lot to write in one month, but your novel may end up being significantly longer than that. The key to meet your November writing goals is to focus on writing without going back and editing what you've written.

## How to Participate

In order to participate, go to the official NaNoWriMo website, which is http://nanowrimo.org/. You can find support from other writers inside the forums. Of course creating an account and accepting the challenge are the first steps.

During November, you can update your word count and win badges for meeting certain milestones. And by the end of November, you'll have to upload your novel to validate your word count in order to be an official NaNoWriMo winner!

One of the best reasons to participate in NaNoWriMo is the added motivation you'll get from joining in this novel-writing adventure with lots of other participants. NaNoWriMo might spur you on to make it to the finish line. On the other hand, if it's December, that doesn't mean you shouldn't write anything until next November comes around. After all, you can institute your own novel writing month during any month of the year.

By the way, writing during that first month can also help you figure out if writing is really what you want to do. In the end, you may decide that having your name in print is not worth all the effort that goes into a writing a book. And that's okay, too. At least, you'll have given it your best shot.

# 7. Join a Writing Support Group

There's no need to wait for National Novel Writing Month to find writing support groups. There are many of them out there. You can start by visiting your local library or searching online groups like meetup.com. And if your area doesn't have a writing support group, you might even want to start your own!

If you live in a bigger town, you'll have the advantage of being able to pick and choose which group you want to join. There'll be groups for different genres, women writers, first-time authors, and maybe even a group of people who publish specifically on Amazon Kindle.

The best writing support group is one that meets in person on a regular basis at least once a month. This gives you some facetime with each other and helps you add accountability. After all, you don't want to go to your next meeting and report that you didn't look at your manuscript at all during the last month, do you? Having a regular meeting is probably the reason why programs like Weight Watchers work. Just showing up is a big step in the right direction.

If you can't find the time to go to a meeting, you can still try joining an online writing group. There are plenty of them on Facebook alone.

Why is joining a writing group so important? Aren't most writers solitary people? They can be, but that doesn't mean we don't enjoy company every once in a while. Plus, it's a good idea to talk to other people with similar views and goals to keep you on track with yours. You might even find inspiration for your next story or receive a recommendation for a new writing tool. However, the main goal is to have fun while you're there!

Some writing groups require you to pay a membership fee. There's nothing wrong with that if belonging to the group is beneficial and helps you with your writing. But even the groups that charge you a fee should let you try it out first. After all, if you don't get along with the members, you're in the wrong group.

# 8. Force Yourself NOT to Edit

One way to ensure that your novel will never get finished is to keep changing and editing the story before you're even halfway through the manuscript. Don't get me wrong. It can be necessary to scrap a story in its entirety or edit a significant portion of it on occasion. But if that's all you ever do, you probably won't finish that novel anytime soon.

One way to avoid getting sucked into editing mode is not to edit at all until you're done writing the entire first draft. Don't scroll through your book each time you sit down to write. Find the spot where you left off and keep going.

This is harder than it sounds, especially when you're suffering from writer's block. It might seem productive to edit since you're not writing anyway, but editing can really backfire on you.

If the book is so bad that you can't continue writing it, you may want to consider starting over with a new story. If you still want to salvage some of your book, you should at least work with an outline to help you move it along.

When it comes to editing, you'll be doing enough of it later on. And you will get so sick of it that you will wish it was time to write again. It's not uncommon to edit a book 20 times or more before it's deemed ready for publication. And those are just your edits. After that, it goes to your editor, your agent, and your publisher....

# 9. Research Small Details Later

When you're writing a nonfiction book, it's easy to get stuck doing research all the time. This is especially true if you're writing a book that requires a lot of statistics, references, and studies. Unfortunately, getting stuck doing research isn't limited to non-fiction writers. Fiction writers can also spend lots of hours digging through the library or surfing the Internet for obscure knowledge.

Yes, it's important to get the small details right. For example, if your story is set in Germany, you can't have your main character go grocery shopping at Walmart on a Sunday afternoon for two reasons. One, Walmart no longer has a presence in Germany. Two, grocery stores are not open on Sundays. (By the way, I know this because I was born and raised in Germany.) That being said, you probably won't get a lot of hate mail when you get it wrong.

It's not a good idea to postpone writing to do your research regardless of how important those details are. If you're not sure about a certain aspect of your story and want to research it further, you should highlight the content and move on. When your first draft is finished, you can declare a research week or month and comb through those highlighted sections.

The thing about doing research all at once instead of in segments is that it will save you time overall. It's the same as when you batch other tasks, such as laundry or doing your bills. Doing research once may only take you 10 hours. If you do research every time you stumble on a little fact, then you may spend many additional hours on getting it done. Part of it is that doing research can easily cause you to get sidetracked. The other part is that you only have to research one thing, so you're probably not very efficient at doing the work.

Instead of batching the research, you could also keep written notes and do the research on your phone while you're waiting around at the doctor's office. However, this requires a little bit more planning and organization on your part, so it may not work for you. Plus, if you're using a novel writing program like Novelize, you can actually work on your story on your phone at the doctor's office. That's even better than researching.

## Designate Research Time

Every novel requires at least some research, even the ones that are almost autobiographical, although research for an autobiographical novel is probably quite minimal. You should definitely plan on dedicating some of your time to research. Why is it so important to do research at all? After all, you're writing fiction, so you should be able to make up the facts as you go along, right? Well, it depends.

Most fiction writers still strive for accuracy. Even when you're writing fiction, you want to be believable. If you mess with too many historical or scientific facts, then that will distract from the story you're trying to tell.

Think about the type of novels you've read recently. If the main character is a lawyer, any job-related details should be accurate or at least believable. If you happen to be a lawyer yourself, it's probably a lot easier to keep the facts straight.

But if you dislike doing research of any kind, you might want to stay away from writing historical fiction. Readers of historical fiction tend to be very knowledgeable about their favorite times in history.

Sci-Fi and fantasy readers are also very detail-oriented. In fact, while you're making up the details, they still need to be believable. And if you're writing 'hard' Sci-Fi, you have to adhere to current scientific knowledge.

Lastly, you may want to stick to writing about locations and professions you personally know and understand. If your character gets chased around the city of Chicago, you should know a little bit about it. You certainly want to avoid misplacing major landmarks.

If you're unsure about certain local customs, it might be a good idea to find a Beta reader with the knowledge you need. That way you can iron out the kinks later. After all, you don't want to risk getting bad reviews because you didn't feel like doing the research, do you? And the people who are sticklers for accuracy will be the first ones to write a bad review.

By the way, most authors still add a disclaimer to their book stating that things presented as facts in the book may not be entirely accurate.

# 10. Always Start with a Plan

There's a huge difference between writing and writing with a plan. When I sit down to write, it's easy for my mind to go blank. And whether you want to call it writer's block or something else, it's not helping me be productive. Fortunately, I know how to fix this problem. I start with a plan.

If you know what's going to happen in your story in broad strokes, you can start making it come alive. It doesn't hurt if you can visualize your characters and move them along, either. But the most important part of writing consistently might be to start with a broad outline.

## Start with a Broad Outline

What is going to happen in your book? Who are the main characters, and what are the big conflicts they're dealing with in your story? You can try to add a little bit of detail at this point, too. What will happen in the beginning, in the middle, and at the end?

The conflict in the story could be a big international crisis, but it could also be the internal conflict your main character is dealing with. Of course you'll need a few major events to move your story along.

## Set Up Your Chapters

Now that you know what will happen in general, it's time to set up your chapters. You don't have to be specific at this point, but you can use one or two sentences to describe what will happen in each chapter.

Outlining the chapters this way can take some time. The middle of your book is probably going to be the most difficult part. After all, you probably know what you want the beginning and ending to look like. In order to get the story moving, you should think about it logically. If you were your main character, what would you do next?

## *Let Your Creative Juices Flow*

Now that you have your broad outline in place, it's time to let your creative juices flow. You don't necessarily have to start at the beginning and work your way through to the end, but many fiction writers probably prefer it that way. Writing from beginning to end helps you keep your story details accurate and avoid putting the cart before the horse.

If you have a good idea overnight for a certain part of your book, feel free to work on that particular chapter or scene. On the days where you don't feel compelled to write a specific part of your book, you can go to the next scene in line and try to continue the story.

# 11. Make a Commitment and Stick to It

If you want to write a book, you have to make a real commitment and stick to it. Of course that's always easier said than done. But did you know that the difference between a wish and a goal is a deadline? A useful goal is also measurable in addition to having a real deadline.

For example, "I want to finish my novel" is not a good New Year's resolution. That's because it's vague. It's almost the same as saying "One day I'll write a book". That day may never come unless you create a real goal and stick to it.

"I will finish my first novel by June 30th" is a good goal. It would be even better if you added a word count to it so you know that you didn't cut your story short. There's nothing wrong with writing a short story as long as that was your intention. To get a good idea of what your word count goal should be, you can refer back to the chapter titled "How Many Words Should Your Book Have" in the beginning of this book.

After you've set your goal, it's time to create a plan on how to achieve the goal. This means you need to figure out when you're going to work on your book. Are you going to wake up early and write in the mornings? Will you write in the evenings instead of watching your favorite TV shows? Are you going to write every day or every other day?

If you want to get your book done, you need to make plans to write. And the more details you include in this plan, the more likely it is that you'll stick to your plan. You may even include details on what to do if you miss a daily goal or if you just don't feel like writing.

Here are the steps you may want to follow:

- Set a deadline
- Set a measurable goal (word or page count works)
- Set baby step goals (for example 500 words a day or 10,000 words by the end of the month)
- Determine when and where you're going to write each day
- Determine how to stick to your writing schedule when you're not motivated
- Determine what you'll do if you miss a day
- Celebrate your achievements
- Keep your progress visible

Making a real commitment to write your book is not difficult as long as you act on it. Talking about it can help, too. Mentioning your goals to your friends and family will keep you motivated, but you also need to keep your goals visible. Record your progress on your bathroom mirror, on your fridge, and on Facebook for good measure.

# 12. Write on the Go

Writing a book is not easy. It takes a lot of determination and time to get it done. Did I mention time? Finding the time to write is probably the hardest aspects of finishing the first draft of your book. If you have a hard time finding the time to write, you might want to consider writing on the go.

## Too Many Distractions at Home

Of course it would be much easier to sit down leisurely at your desk and write. But as soon as you get home from work, there are a million other things to attend to: laundry, dishes, and your kids' homework. By the time your evening chores are done all you'll want to do is sit down and watch TV. Of course some people write a lot better at night. If you're a night owl and do your best work at night, that's when you should write. For the rest of us, it's important to take advantage of the time we have available during the day, even if that time is few and far between.

## Use Idle Time Effectively

Think about how many minutes and hours you waste waiting around for things to happen? What do you normally do while you're waiting in line to return an item, sitting in the doctor's waiting room, or riding the bus to work? What about all those hours you sit around waiting for your car to get an oil change? Do you daydream, read, or watch other people trying to guess what they're up to?

Why don't you use some of that waiting time to write your novel instead? With Novelize, you can even write your novel on your phone wherever you are as long as you have an Internet connection.

## *Every Minute Counts*

You don't have to designate 8 hours each day to write, although if you can, that's awesome. Most writers get their first book done on a part-time basis. When it comes to writing, every minute counts. Even if you only spend 15 minutes each day waiting around, that's over 1 1/2 hours of writing time if you use this opportunity to work on your novel instead. You can accomplish quite a bit in an hour and a half even if it's interrupted writing time.

# 13. Write in Short Bursts

One of the biggest problems writers face is that there is never enough time to write. But maybe the problem isn't that there isn't enough time to write, but that you don't have large chunks of time to devote to writing. For example, you may have 30 minutes before it's time to pick up the kids from school, 15 minutes until the pizza is done, or 20 minutes until your partner comes to pick you up for a lunch date.

The thing is you can use every one of those intervals to write. Of course it would be better if you had a whole hour instead of 3 separate chunks of time, but your book doesn't care how it gets written. It's time to use those 15-minute intervals and become more productive.

You can get a lot done in 15 minutes. It's worth trying! And the best part is that if you start something and really get into it, you'll be more likely to find more time to write later in the day. In fact, you might be finishing the rest of your story in your head while you're running the next errand. As long as you're still paying attention to the road while you're driving, that's awesome. So you see that having little chunks of time quickly adds up and helps get your book done faster.

Even if you're not currently in the mood to work on your story, you can easily create a few new characters for your novel in 15 minutes. You could also do some quick research on the location you've chosen for your book. You could finish outlining the last few chapters. Or you could proofread the first one. There are lots of things you can accomplish in 15 minutes. And if you can type fast, you could easily write 500 words in that timeframe. Why don't you give it a try?

# 14. Schedule Time Off and Take a Break

So far the focus of this book has been about finding time to write. But now I have to admit that you have to take time off from writing on occasion. You already know that it's going to take several months to finish your book. That's a long time to work every day without taking a break.

The good news is that taking time off from writing can actually make you more productive when you go back to it. That's why most of us take 2 days off after working 5, and that's why we all need to take vacations throughout the year. Recharging your batteries will make you a happier and more productive person all around. It's also quite possible that you'll have a few more creative brainstorms when you're not writing.

By the way, nobody says that you're required to take a day off. However, if you're not feeling as productive as you normally are, maybe that's a sign that you need to step back. You also don't have to take 2 days off in a row. You could take a break on Wednesdays and Saturdays instead. If writing is not your full-time job, you may also need to take more than 2 days off each week.

And if you've finished writing a book, you may want to take an extended time off before you start the editing process. In fact, taking a break makes your editing better because you're starting with a fresh set of eyes. Of course you can always start writing a new book during that time, but there's nothing wrong with basking in your accomplishment for a little while before going back to work. You deserve it!

# 15. Minimize Distractions

Whenever you sit down to write, you need to minimize distractions. While you have no influence over when your neighbor decides to mow the lawn, you can turn off your phone and close your email program while you're writing. And when it comes to loud neighbors or your own kids, you can always invest in a good set of earplugs.

If you find that you get distracted easily, you need to make a list of what's keeping you from writing. Is it the fact that you haven't done the dishes, the instant messages on Facebook, or your kids who come and talk to you every few minutes while you're in the middle of killing the villain of your story?

Depending on what's distracting you, there are different ways to deal with it. If you're one of those people who can't stand having a dirty kitchen, you'll have to do the dishes first. When it comes to phones, email, Facebook, etc., you just need to turn everything off. Chances are no deaths will result from the fact that you have temporarily disconnected from the world.

For children, pets, partners, and other obligations that seem to pounce on you whenever you sit down to write, you'll have to be firm. If you make the rule that you need to be undisturbed when you're writing, you need to enforce it, too. If your kids are too young to understand the concept, you might need to close the door to your office.

By the way, I'm not asking you to ignore your kids. It's important that they're taken care of and that they get to spend some quality time with you. When kids are younger, it's best to spend time with them first before disengaging and letting them run off on their own. Above all, it should never become a habit to blow off your kids with "not right now" when they need you. In fact, they probably need you more than you need to write that book.

But (you knew there was going to be a but) you also need to have some time to yourself. I'm assuming that you don't come home from work, shut yourself in your office to write, and go to bed without talking to your partner or your kids. In that case, my advice to you is to focus on what really matters: it's not your book. But for most of us, work and family demand all of our attention throughout the day. There's absolutely nothing wrong with taking a breather and doing something for you. In fact, you'll be happier because of it, and you'll enjoy being around your kids and partner more. And they'll like you better when you're happy, too.

# 16. Say No

In order to say "yes" to writing your book, you're going to have to say "no" to a lot of other things. For example, that new TV show you wanted to watch? If you're serious about writing and have only very limited time to do it, you may want to postpone that indefinitely. Similarly, if you're currently swamped with work, you need to make a decision. Is working overtime in the long run better than writing your book and spending time with your family?

It's quite possible that working is helping you advance in your career, which is a good long-term goal. However, I'm always skeptical when people sacrifice their daily happiness for something that won't benefit them for many years to come if at all.

Time is limited for all of us. If you don't spend time writing your book, you will use your time for something else. There's nothing wrong with it, but it's something that you should be aware of. Time is a limited resource even more so than money, and they're not making any more of it for you.

Learning to say "no" can be difficult for some people. I understand it can be hard, because you may be used to pleasing people and participating in what everyone else is doing. Personally, I felt bad about declining to sell Girl Scout cookies with my daughters even though we're part of the troop. The toughest part was watching the other girls receive prizes and awards for cookie sales while my daughters felt a little left out.

But when it comes down to it, I don't want to spend several hours in the evenings and weekends standing at a booth in front of our local grocery store. And I'm glad I said "no". The girls enjoy our family activities much more than they would have liked selling cookies. And those prizes their friends received are about as cool as the toys you can buy at the Dollar Store.

Saying "no" takes practice if you're not used to saying it. But it can be extremely liberating. Try it today. The next time somebody asks you to do something you don't want to do, say no. If you don't feel comfortable politely declining, you can suggest an alternative. You don't always have to give a reason for declining, but you can if you want to.

Here are a few suggestions on how to say no, but feel free to come up with your own!

"No thanks. I already have other plans."

"No, I can't meet you today. But I'll see you at the meeting on Wednesday."

"No, I don't want to do the grocery shopping, but I'll help you write up a shopping list."

"No, you can't get ice-cream, but you can have a yogurt."

"No, I can't play right now, but I'll help you build a tower as soon as I'm done writing this chapter."

"No, I don't want to buy any cookies because I'm on a diet. But you could ask my neighbor, she loves cookies."

If you're not feeling comfortable saying no, you could use the copout "maybe". However, most people know that "maybe" usually means "no". And you'll probably respect yourself more if you learn to politely decline the invitation instead of pretending that you'll think about it.

# 17. Pick the Right Project

For some people the problem isn't necessarily finding the time to write but finding the right project to work on. Maybe you work as a ghostwriter, publish articles for a magazine, host your own blog, and also have an unfinished novel waiting for your attention. It can be difficult to figure out what you should be working on next.

You could try to complete one project at a time, allowing you to dedicate all of your time, resources, and energy to the one you're currently working on. That's probably the best idea, except for the fact that some projects don't pay as well as others. For example, if you ghostwrite for a living, you can't put that on hold while you write a novel for fun.

## Designate Specific Days

Another option is to alternate working on different projects throughout the week. You might designate specific days or times to work on one project instead of another. During the week, you could spend your days on your day job and write articles for publication. On the weekend, you might decide to switch and spend some time working on your own blog or novel or both.

What if you feel more creative during the week? After all, your ghostwriting has to get done in order for you to pay the bills, so chances are you'll get it done on the weekend if necessary. Is it feasible for you to work on a little bit of both each day?

Here is what your week might look like:

- Monday: Ghostwriting 5,000 words
- Tuesday: 2 blog articles for your blog, 1,000 words for your novel
- Wednesday: Ghostwriting 5,000 words, 1 blog article for your blog
- Thursday: Ghostwriting 5,000 words
- Friday: Research and write magazine article
- Saturday: Ghostwriting 1,000 words, editing chapter in your novel
- Sunday: Time to take a break and go hiking

Obviously, this is an example and the word counts are completely random. You can obviously work more or less depending on what needs to get done in order for you to earn a living and spend time with your family on top of it. The thing is that you don't have to work Monday through Friday if you don't want to.

I like scheduling activities with my kids throughout the week. Since we're homeschooling, we can take advantage of going places without the crowds that way. Therefore, I prefer staying home on weekends and using some of that time to write.

## Set Multiple Weekly Goals

Another approach is to set weekly word count goals for however many projects you're juggling at one time. As soon as you reach the goal for one project, it's time to switch to the next one. That way you'll make progress on all fronts and leave nothing behind.

Here is what your weekly goals might look like:

- Ghostwriting: 15,000 words
- Research and write one magazine article
- Write 3,000 words on your novel
- Edit 1 chapter of your novel
- Write and schedule 3 new blog posts

It's a good idea to know ahead of time what you want to accomplish each week. This way you're not staring at the computer wondering what you should work on. Of course you might feel more inclined to work on your novel instead of researching a magazine article, but you still have to meet all of your goals. Once you've written 3,000 words in your novel, it's time to switch and reach your other goals. Of course you can still write additional words in your novel at the end of the week provided everything else got done, too.

You may combine the weekly goals and the daily schedule by assigning daily goals for yourself, too. But you don't have to micromanage your writing unless it helps you get things done. Personally, I love checking off things on my to-do list, so I tend to write down what I want to get done beforehand. Plus, without my to-do list I spend way too much time on Facebook or surfing the Internet…

## *18. Get Out of Your Rut*

It can be beneficial to write outside of your office for a nice change of scenery. You don't even have to leave your house if you don't want to. Sometimes it's enough to get you out of your rut by writing in a different room.

Here are a few suggestions for new writing locations:

- At the library
- At the Zoo
- Next to the flower beds at the Botanical garden
- On a bench at the park
- On the bus
- By the pool
- In your backyard
- In your closet
- On your front porch
- At a coffee shop
- At the museum
- At the aquarium
- Inside the shopping mall
- On your bed
- At a friend's house
- On a boat or ferry
- At the campground
- At your kitchen table
- Inside the chicken coop

- Inside a tree house

Don't let this list stop you from finding other, more exciting places to write. My imagination won't take me as far as your imagination might take you. The only requirement your writing place has to meet is that you have to like it. It should be comfortable enough to allow you to write for extended periods of time, too. Plus, there's absolutely nothing stopping you from taking a pillow or blanket along.

The great thing about writing in a different location than the one you normally choose is that it may spark your creativity. That's one of the reasons people enjoy redecorating their home or moving their furniture around.

It's also possible that writing in another location has a calming effect on you. After all, you're not there to see the dirty dishes in the sink. And you're not reminded of your to-do-list that includes grocery shopping, cleaning the bathroom, and paying bills. Finally, if you end up writing outside, you might be in a better frame of mind just because the sun is shining on your face and there is a nice breeze in the air.

The best part about changing where you write is that your creativity boost will last for a while. That means writing at the park once a month could be enough to get you out of your rut. Of course you shouldn't let that stop you from switching things up more often than that.

## 19. Find a Writing Partner

Do you need a writing partner in order to finish your novel? Not really, but it can't hurt. You should find someone else who is at least as motivated to write as you are. If I tried to team up with my husband (who has lots of ideas for different stories but hasn't written any of them down), I'd never finish a book. On the other hand, seeing me write has motivated him several times to start a new book.

In order for your writing partner to keep you motivated to write, you need to communicate with him or her on a regular basis. This could be a weekly phone call or a Skype meeting. Of course you're free to meet in person as well if time and location allow this. In fact, it could be great to meet up to write so you can both add more words to each of your stories.

In a way, writing is a solitary occupation. But it can be comforting to have someone who is doing the same thing. A writing partner is more than just an accountability partner. They can help you overcome problems with your story, act as a sounding board, and be one of your first Beta readers.

If you can get a group of people together, that might be even more beneficial. After all, one partner can always bail out. Either they're sick or just too busy to write, or they just don't feel like writing this week. If there is a whole group of writers, there will always be someone who is pushing you on. There will always be one person who is a step or two ahead of you, which can help you get going. There will always be people who have written less than you, too. This helps counterbalance the fact that you may never write as much as the top achievers.

Finding a group is probably not too difficult, but it might be harder to find a local group you can meet up in person with. It's a good idea to come to a meeting and get to know the other writers before you commit to becoming part of the group. It's important that you find partners who will be supportive of you, wherever you are in your writing process. Finally, you should probably get along with them personally, too.

Some people will argue that they don't have time to join a writing group. If they had time to join such a group, they'd have time to write. The thing is that joining a writing group may help you find the time to write. Knowing that you'll be sharing your writing successes at the next meeting can be enough motivation to write more often.

## *When You Don't Have Time to Meet*

Since you're already having difficulties finding the time to write, you may wonder why I would suggest meeting up with other writers in person. Obviously, you're too busy for that. Fortunately, you can still meet up with other people from the comfort of your own home. Actually, you don't even have to meet up with them in order to take advantage of being part of a writing group.

You can find online groups or forums to interact with. Some writing groups have very active moderators that encourage group members to write every single day. So if your writing group is the first thing you check on Facebook, you might just close Facebook and work on your book instead. I've actually done that a few times.

An online writing group can also give you some valuable feedback. Many members will respond very quickly to questions or requests.

Choosing an online group is similar to choosing a group that meets in person. You still want to find a group that shares your goals to get the most out of it. Plus, you'll probably also want a group where the members are nice to each other and refrain from spamming each other with offers to buy something.

## *20. Participate in a Contest*

I'm sure you heard of weight-loss contests before. Many organizations decide to host these competitions regularly to encourage their employees to lose unwanted pounds. In fact, your office might host similar contests on occasion. Participating in a contest is a great idea because it spurs everyone on to do their best. That's why you might want to consider joining a writing contest.

It doesn't have to be as big or as popular as National Novel Writing Month. It could be a small contest hosted by your local newspaper. It could even be a contest that you've started yourself.

The type of writing contest I'd like you to participate in should focus on getting you to write. The winner should be the one who has written the highest number of words. Why is that better than awarding the prize to the writer with the best book?

The answer is pretty simple: it's easier. In order to reward the best book, you would need to set someone up as a judge. Judging different stories is always subjective. However, you can't argue with word count just like you can't argue with number of pounds lost. The point of the contest is to get you writing. You can edit the book later.

## Get Some Skin in the Game

Now we all know how easy it is to join a weight-loss contest. Some offices don't even ask if you want to participate. Your name is on the list because you work there. But in order for the challenge to work for you, you should get some skin in the game. Generally, this means you need to place a bet.

If you're earning minimum wage, betting $20 may be a lot of money to you. It would hurt to lose 20 bucks since you have to work for 3 hours to earn it back. But if you can get 5 people to participate in the contest, each of you stands to win $100. That's nothing to laugh at. Of course, if spending $20 on a bet doesn't make you nervous, you might need to raise the stakes.

By the way, I'm not implying that you should take up gambling. However, when you join a writing contest, you actually have a true chance of winning. Better yet, you can directly influence whether you'll win or not by getting some words on paper. Plus, the odds are much better than at the lottery or on the racetrack.

Last but not least, even the people who don't win aren't losers. After all, the contest will spur you on to write something. That might be worth the money tenfold. And now that you have the beginning of a story, you can use other techniques in this book to help you find the time to finish it.

# 21. Unplug from TV, Netflix & Co.

Do you know how much time the average American spends watching TV every week? Actually, the numbers vary based on which study you read. However, the consensus is that most people watch between 2 and 5 hours of TV every day. That's 14 to 35 hours a week. Some people watch even more than that!

The numbers are more shocking when you think about the fact that watching TV essentially takes up the same amount of time as a part-time or even a full-time job. However, it doesn't come with any of the same benefits. Watching TV doesn't make you feel fulfilled, and it certainly doesn't pay well.

The problem is that turning on the TV is a lot easier than going for a jog, reading a book, or writing a novel. It's also one of the cheapest 'activities' you can do as a family. Unfortunately, most of us watch TV mindlessly. If you specifically turn on the TV to watch a documentary or a funny movie, that would be understandable. And doing that isn't a bad way to spend your leisure time, either. Unfortunately, most TV watching is mindless. You may end up staring at the screen for hours without getting anything out of it.

The easiest answer is to unplug. Try it for a week. Better yet, try it for a whole month. Your family might be bored and annoyed for the first few days, but then something magical will happen. You might get out a board game. You might decide to go for a walk in the evening. You might spend a lot more time talking to your partner. And you might finally write that novel. Another benefit to unplugging: you save a little bit of money on your cable bill or Netflix etc.

If your family won't cooperate with unplugging the TV, you can at least institute TV-free days or evenings. If your family is resentful at first, you should plan alternative activities that you can do together in the beginning. You could read fairy tales or tell each other stories about your day. Life is too short to watch too much TV.

## *22. Turn Your Phone Off*

When I was growing up, cell phones were just becoming popular. Now I see elementary school kids running around with expensive Smartphones. You may think that I'm against technology, and my husband might confirm this, but our dependency on electronics has truly gotten out of hand.

As far as writing your book is concerned, turning your phone off on occasion can't hurt. In fact, you probably don't even realize how much time you spend calling, texting, or surfing the web for unimportant information.

Yes, it's nice to have a phone when you need directions to a store you don't go to very often. But you don't need to text on your phone the entire time you're pushing your kid on the swing. Nor do you need to surf the Internet while you're having a date with your partner.

If you always keep your phone on for work-related reasons, that's going to cause you to feel resentment and experience burnout before too long. In the meantime, feeling like you're on call the entire time will increase your stress levels dramatically. Unless you get paid to be on call 24/7, I recommend turning your work phone off after normal business hours. Chances are nobody is going to notice.

When you're sitting down to work on your novel, you should turn your phone off. At the very least, silence your ringer so that you don't get distracted every time somebody sends you a text message or email. If you are expecting an important call or want to be available for the babysitter or your spouse, you can program your phone to let certain calls go through while silencing the rest. If your phone can't do that or you can't figure out how, you'll need to screen your calls the old-fashioned way.

# 23. Examine Your Family Obligations

While you get to choose your friends, you don't get to choose your family. Of course having family members nearby is often an advantage especially if they'll babysit your kids for free. On the other hand, many grownups spend more time complaining about their family, a lot of times their in-laws, than their jobs.

Family obligations can be very time-consuming. This is true when you have a very large family and when some of your family members need a lot of attention. I'm not suggesting that you should stop visiting grandma at the nursing home because you want to get your novel written. And if one of your loved ones is seriously ill, then your priorities will also need to shift accordingly.

However, there are some family obligations that may not be that important to you. Yet you're expected to go. Whether it's your cousin's daughter's nephew's wedding or your aunt's house warming party doesn't really matter. If you don't get along with the majority of your family members attending the event, it may be time to cut the cord.

Here is the hard truth: you can live your life only once. You're not going to regret missing out on family reunions that involved a lot of tension and unpleasantness. Instead, you should spend time with the family members who mean something to you, whether you're closely related or not. Incidentally, you could easily finish another chapter in your novel instead of attending monthly family feuds.

## 24. Log Your Hours

Do you want to know how you spend the 24 yours you have each day? I strongly suggest keeping a time diary for a week, but 2 or 3 weeks is even better. For most people, this is an eye-opening experience. You may not realize how much time you spend on activities that aren't meaningful to you, whether that's cooking, cleaning, or shuttling the kids to after-school activities.

I'm not going to reinvent the wheel here. Laura Vanderkam already does a fabulous job of helping people manage their time. You can download her PDF or Excel worksheet and log how you spend your hours each day. The more often you record what you're doing, the more accurate your time log will be.

Here is the link to the website: http://lauravanderkam.com/books/168-hours/manage-your-time/.

Of course the reason you want to log your hours in the first place is that you need to figure out what you're doing with your time. Afterwards, you can brainstorm how you can spend it better. Logging your time will help you determine which tasks you're spending too much time on and where you can squeeze in some time to write your book.

## Chapter 11

## *One Tip that Will Change Your Life*

By now you've read a lot of different suggestions to help you find the time to write your novel. Many of them will work for you, and you probably already identified which ones you're going to try first. But all in all, it might still be a little overwhelming. How are you going to remember from day to day what you can to do increase the time you spend on writing your novel?

I'm so glad you asked. To make it all easier for you, I have one tip for you that may change your life. By the way, this applies to all of your activities, not just writing your novel. Are you ready for the tip? Here it is:

**You have to learn to differentiate between the urgent and important and do the important things first.**

Simple, isn't it? Before you work on a new task, you should understand whether you're working on something urgent or important. Few tasks fall in both categories.

The idea of differentiating between urgent and important things is not new. Former U.S. President Dwight D. Eisenhower organized his workload and priorities in the following order:

1.  Urgent and important
2.  Important but not urgent
3.  Not important but urgent
4.  Not important and not urgent

This concept was later made popular by Steven Covey's "7 Habits of Highly Effective People". Of course, anything that's neither important nor urgent is generally a time waster, such as most emails. You should avoid doing these types of tasks as much as you can by eliminating them, outsourcing them, and practicing selective ignorance.

Urgent tasks that are not important also need to be scrutinized further. Can you delegate them or get rid of them? You may have to revisit the chapter on saying no to get some of these things off your to-do list.

The thing about urgent tasks is that they always get done because they have to. You're going to do your job because your boss is breathing down your neck. You're going to go grocery shopping because the kids are hungry for dinner. You're going to get gas for your car because if you don't, you'll run out and get stuck on the side of the road.

The problem is that we spend so much time taking care of seemingly urgent tasks that we don't do what's truly important to us. Let's illustrate with an example.

You're out of milk and eggs and other groceries you deem essential. Instead of running off to the grocery store right away (urgent), you should spend some time on doing the important thing first: creating a menu for the week and a shopping list. Technically, you don't need either to go grocery shopping, but having them will make your trip much easier and more efficient. Plus, you'll probably eliminate additional trips to the store for the rest of the week.

## 11.1 Label Your To-Do-List

You have to realize that it's going to take you some time to recognize the difference between urgent and important activities. You won't always be able to do the important ones first especially if some activities are truly urgent.

In order to use your time effectively, you should prepare a list of things you need to get done before you start your day. You can even prepare that list on the evening beforehand. After your to-do-list is done, you need to go through the list and mark each items as either important or urgent.

Just knowing which items are truly important will make you pay more attention to them that day.

When it comes to writing, you're going to have to get into the habit of doing it before you're doing other things that overwhelm you.

## 11.2 Stop and Ask Yourself a Question

Another strategy you should follow throughout the day is to stop and ask yourself the following question:

### Is what I'm currently doing urgent or important?

Again, you won't be able to ignore all of the urgent things on your to-do-list. That's not my intention. However, you shouldn't overestimate the importance of the things you're doing. Just because something is urgent doesn't mean it's worth spending a lot of your time on.

# Chapter 12:

# Which Strategy Will Work for You?

You obviously don't need to use every strategy from the previous chapters to write your book. The best thing to do is to pick one and go with it. At the end of this chapter, you'll find a quick summary of the strategies you can apply to finding the time to write. If you don't care which one you should try first, then I recommend you close your eyes and pick one.

But now there should be no more excuses for you. Ready? Set...Write!

## *12.1. Summary of Strategies to Keep You Writing*

- o   Set a designated time
- o   Set a minimum word requirement
- o   Use reward (or punishment)
- o   Participate in NaNoWriMo
- o   Join a support group
- o   Force yourself not to edit
- o   Research small details later
- o   Always start with a plan
- o   Make a commitment and stick to it
- o   Write on the go
- o   Write in short bursts
- o   Schedule time off and take a break
- o   Minimize distractions
- o   Say no
- o   Pick the right project
- o   Get out of your rut
- o   Find a writing partner
- o   Participate in a Contest
- o   Unplug from TV, Netflix & Co.
- o   Turn your phone off
- o   Examine your family obligations
- o   Log your hours
- o   Always do the important things first

# Please Review this Book

As a self-published author, I need your help. If you liked this book, please take a moment to review it on Amazon. I'd also love to hear your questions, comments, and feedback. You can email me directly at anita@getnovelize.com.

# About the Author

Anita Evensen writes articles and books because she feels compelled to write whenever she can. She's also passionate about natural childbirth and homeschooling. She lives in Texas with her husband and their 4 children. In her free time, she likes to read and do puzzles.

Anita founded Novelize (www.getnovelize.com) with her husband. Novelize is a novel writing app designed to keep you on track with your writing goals.